WIN AT THE CASINO

WIN AT THE CASINO

BY DENNIS R. HARRISON

FELL PUBLISHERS, INC.
Hollywood, Florida

International Standard Book Number: 0-8119-0656-6

Library of Congress Catalog Card Number: 82-071742

For information address:
Fell Publishers, Inc.
2131 Hollywood Blvd.
Hollywood, FL 33020

Published simultaneously in Canada by Prentice-Hall Canada, Toronto, Canada

Manufactured in the United States of America
1234567890

CONTENTS

WIN AT THE CASINO

INTRODUCTION

If you are one of those people who does not care whether you win or lose at the casino of your choice, you do not need to read this book. If you are a professional gambler, you do not need to read this book. If you have a need or a psychological compulsion to lose money, you do not need to read this book. If you enjoy the idea of giving your money to the casinos, of making a willful donation in exchange for a few free drinks and a "good" time, you do not need to read this book.

However, if you would like to be one of the lucky few who actually win money, reading this book can help. I cannot guarantee you will beat the casinos at every turn of the cards, every roll of the dice, or every spin of the wheel. But, if you listen to what I have to say and apply a few of my general principles, you will reduce your losses and begin the arduous journey leading to consistent success.

This book covers the major games offered in casinos: Blackjack, Craps, Roulette, Baccarat, Keno and Slot Machines. But, before we can discuss these games, we must consider a few general ideas which can help you enormously.

First, I would like to talk about attitude. No, I'm not going to suggest that you enroll in a Dale Carnegie course. Neither am I promoting Norman Vincent Peale or any other author who claims that you can change your life with the proper attitude. But consider for a moment what took place when you decided to visit Las Vegas, Lake Tahoe, Reno, or Atlantic City. You called your friendly travel agent to arrange the three day/two night venture and paid in advance. You found a neighbor to feed the dog and cat, perhaps talked a few friends into joining you. Then, before you left your home town, you engaged in a small amount of soul searching, and decided how much money you could afford to lose. Am I right?

Maybe you decided on $200, $1000, or more. The amount makes no difference. For the purpose of my point we'll assume you decided on $500. You determined that losing $500 would not "kill" you would still be able to pay the bills when you returned home, and the $500 was really "fun" money, anyway.

I'm not saying you were wrong. You simply experienced the same thought process as have millions of other people and reached the same conclusions. But think about it for a moment. Your first assumption about the trip was that you were going to *lose* money. Now I ask you, how far would you have gotten with your life if you had always assumed that you would lose?

And why did you make the "losing" assumption in the first place? The reasons are numerous — here are a few:

- You've heard of all the various games of chance, but you don't really understand them, so how could you possibly expect to win?
- People always lose. The gambling/casino business is prospering because *everbody* loses.
- Only "lucky" people ever win anything, and you've never been lucky.
- The people you know who claim the won money always tend to exaggerate, so you have never believed their preposterous stories.

Believe me — if you thought of any of these reasons, you are not alone. Nearly every person I've interviewed assumed that he or she would lose money. And nearly all of those people were correct. Nearly all of them did, in fact, lose money.

But what happens when you *don't* expect to lose? What happens when you actually, God forbid, expect to win? Will you acquire enormous amounts of money? No. Will you return home with all the money that you brought? Maybe.

I am not saying a change of attitude will make you a winner, but a change of attitude can help. Coupled with other basic truths contained in this book, a better attitude *will* help you become a winner.

Assuming you will lose your $500 is not the way to start your trip. Do you really want to lose that $500? Of course not. Do the casinos want to take your $500? Absolutely not. Surprised? You shouldn't be. Think about it. The casinos do not want you returning to Iowa, or New York, or California, without any money. If you lose your entire gambling stake, you may never come back to gamble again, and that's bad for business. The casinos would like you to lose money, but not all of it, not even a majority of it. They would like you to lose half, or a quarter, or even ten percent, but not all of it.

In point of fact, the perfect scenario for the casinos would be something like this: You arrive late Friday afternoon to begin your three day/two night vacation. You brought $500 for gambling. You check into your hotel, gamble until two o'clock in the morning, and lose $175 trying your luck at a potpourri of Roulette, Slots, Craps and Blackjack. Saturday you lose another $40 playing Keno and Roulette. Saturday night, after the dinner show, you drop another $140 at the Crap tables before deciding you're a born loser. It takes all the courage you can muster to avoid severe depression, since you only have $145 left and your plane does not leave until three o'clock Sunday afternoon. It's decision time. Do you risk the rest of your gambling fund in an attempt to recoup your losses? Or do you play Keno for a dollar a game to while away the remaining hours of your stay?

Your thought process goes like this: Damn it, I came here expecting to lose $500. So far I've only lost $355. What the hell? It's only money. Some people bet more than $145 on one hand of Blackjack. I might as well go for broke.

You can't sleep very well Saturday night, so you're up at sunrise. After a quick breakfast, a return to the Crap tables puts $30 winnings into your pockets. A whirl at Roulette proves fruitful when your favorite number comes up on your very last bet. You then win another $80, lose back part of it, but have the presence of mind to walk away from the spinning wheel with $50 of the Casino's money. A try at Blackjack proves frustrating, but another stop at a Crap game nets you another $65. Now, instead of only $145, you have $290 and you're positively convinced your luck has changed.

Unfortunately, a glance at your watch discloses that your bus to the airport leaves in ten minutes. You don't want to leave yet. So, even though you risk missing the bus, you pause at the exit doors to transfer three quarters from your pocket into a slot machine. The result? You hit a $150 payoff and leave town with $440.

You're elated because you "won" $295 on the last day of your stay. You can't wait to come back again. The casino is happy too, since you'll probably return to lose another $60. A casino has millions of visitors each year. If each visitor only loses $60...well, the totals are staggering. In 1979, according to the Tourism Division of the Las Vegas Convention Center, over $4,000,000,000 was lost to Las Vegas casinos.

Now the critical question: Were you a winner or a loser? If your answer is a loser, you're not being completely honest with yourself. Sure, you brought $500 and left town with only $440. Yes, you actually lost $60. But what did you tell your friends when you got home? Probably something like this: "I had a bad streak when I first got there, but I won like crazy on the last day. I only wish I could have stayed a few more days. How did I do, overall? Oh, I think I finished about even. And I hit a $150 jackpot on the slot machines!"

Did you lie? Of course not. You're happy because you didn't lose all your money, and you *did* win on your last day.

What I have just described may be a perfect scenario for the casinos, but it is not a good one for you. For, on your next visit, you are not going to lose *any* money. And if you thought you had a good time even when you lost a little, think about what a good time you'll have if you win.

So your first step is to assume you can win. Then what?

Here comes the hard part. In order to actually win, you must take the time to learn something about the games you're going to play. You must avoid the stupid bets, stay away from the games where the odds are stacked against you, and sidestep the awaiting pitfalls. You must understand the chances of success or failure at each game and plan accordingly. Is that reasonable? Yes! Is that intelligent? You bet!!

Now you're making progress. You're going to assume that you can win and you're going to learn the games. However, a good attitude and a little knowledge of each game will do nothing more than get you into trouble. The old adage about a little knowledge being dangerous is particularly true with gambling. What you really need is *indepth* knowledge of all the games.

But this raises another question. Is it reasonable to believe that you can become "expert" in all the games? No. Can you become expert in one? Yes! You may prefer Craps or Roulette, Baccarat or Blackjack. Whichever your choice, it does not matter. The point is that you must study your choice. This book will teach you the basics of all the major games and either give you tips on how to win or tips on how not to lose. After reading this book you still might lose, but you won't lose as much as most people, and you'll be able to avoid disaster. But you must choose one of the games as your specialty.

My forte is Blackjack. I've studied it extensively, I play it with the confidence that stems from knowledge and experience. I have lost money playing Blackjack on only two occasions. I lost money on my very first visit to Las Vegas, a trip made at a time when I had no knowledge of the game; I also lost at another time when I was trying to impress a few relatives with my expertise. But excluding those two occasions, I have never lost money playing Blackjack. Yes, I have played more than twice.

Am I lucky? No, not particularly, no more so than you. And if my statement about never losing sounds too ludicrous to accept, let me explain.

I normally visit the various gambling meccas for two to five days at a time. During these vacations, I have lost money at Blackjack for an hour, for a day, and even for several days. I have lost for one day, won for three; I have lost for three days, won for one. One time I lost for an incredible ninety hours and only won for six, but I still left town with winnings instead of losses. On various trips I have won as little as three and a half dollars, as much as several thousand dollars. To me, the amount I win has little importance. The key point, in my mind, is that winning money is vastly preferable to losing it. And, the reason that I win is that I *know* how to play Blackjack.

Okay. You select the game of your choice. Now, yet another question presents itself. Is it reasonable to assume that you will play *only* your specialty, to the exclusion of all the other games, for your entire trip? Can you avoid the temptation to pop a few coins in a slot machine, control the urge to wager on your favorite number at Roulette? Can you ignore those joyful cries emanating from the Crap tables? I doubt it. Even if you know that you'll lose, you'll still want to test your luck. But it is *how* you play the games that will determine whether you leave town with winnings or losses.

A winning attitude and in-depth knowledge of your specialty must be combined with rational, intelligent money management. Here's what I suggest: After you determine the size of your gambling fund, divide it into two groups. Group A should be at least eighty percent of the fund, to be used *only* on the game that you have mastered. Group B, the other twenty percent or less, can then be used to experiment with the other games, to test your luck, or to help pass time between your serious gambling sessions. In other words, plan on playing seriously with at least eighty percent of your funds and using the rest on whatever strikes your fancy. And under no circumstances should you ever use any of your serious money to supplement the loss of fun money. Once the fun money is gone, it is gone; so use it sparingly.

If your gambling fund is $500, you would gamble with $400, toy with $100. Who knows what may happen? Perhaps while playing with your fun money you'll win a jackpot at the slot machines or hit your lucky number five times in succession at Roulette. If that happens, great! But don't count on it.

Remember this: The casinos win the majority of their money from players who do not have the slightest idea of what they are doing. And they win the rest of their money because the odds are stacked so badly against the players that it is almost impossible to win. Consequently, you must do three things before you can start on the road to success.

1) You must assume that you will win. 2) You must master the game of your choice. 3) You must have a money management system, and you must stick to that system, no matter what happens.

If you can take these three simple steps, you will be better off than ninety percent of the people whom you see in Las Vegas or any of the other gambling meccas. You can join the elite ten percent who consistently win money.

Now, a word of caution. Strange things happen to perfectly reasonable human beings when they walk into a casino. The man who won't bet more than ten cents back home at the local monthly poker club is seized by a fit of frenzy and finds himself betting $25 on a single hand of Blackjack. The grandmother from Iowa who thought gambling was the "devil's handiwork" drops $300 playing the nickel lot machines. The person who normally follows a religious routine of rest and exercise sits at a Roulette table for 94 consecutive hours. People become obsessed and possessed. Don't let it happen to you.

Take frequent breaks from the action. Use those lavish swimming pools that the hotels built for your use. Enjoy a short nap each afternoon. Go to the lounge shows. In short, do anything to take your mind off gambling. No one can gamble intelligently for long time periods. Do your gambling in sessions lasting no more than an hour or two at a time. This is just as essential as the three steps we discussed earlier.

Good luck and good reading.

1

BLACKJACK

I BEGIN WITH BLACKJACK for two very simple reasons: 1) The odds can be more favorable for the player than in any other game. 2) It is my personal specialty.

To my mind, anyone who does not select Blackjack as his or her specialty is a masochist. The game is simple to play; the rules are clear and understandable. Properly played, the odds can actually be turned to the player's advantage.

I'll start with a basic description of the game. Some authors indicate that, if you already know the basics, you should skip over this section and go on to the next, but I disagree. Even if you already know how the game is played, or *think* you know, read this section. It can't hurt and it might help. I will assume that you are entering a casino for the first time and want to try your luck at Blackjack.

Your first step is to find a table. Not just any table,

but a table where the game is being played for stakes you can tolerate. It is quite embarrassing to rush up to a table, ask for $20 in chips, and then discover that the minimum bet at that table is $100.

You will usually find a small sign, to the dealer's right or left, which will indicate the minimum and maximum allowable wagers at that table. If the sign is obscured by ashtrays and empty drinks, don't hesitate to approach the dealer and inquire directly. Or, simply check the bets being made by the players. If all you see are green chips, it is probably a $25 table (the minimum bet is $25). If all you see are red chips, it is undoubtedly a $5 table. If you see silver dollars or silver dollar tokens, it could be $1, $2, or $3 table. Assuming that you are a novice, you'll want to start with low stakes; if your hotel casino does not offer a low-minimum table, go somewhere else.

This, however, may pose a problem, particularly if you are gambling in Atlantic City, where you may have trouble finding even a $5 table. If, in fact, you want to start the learning process with bets of less than $5, you would be better off planning a vacation to Las Vegas, Reno or Lake Tahoe, where $2 and even $1 tables may still be found with ease, especially during the week.

Figure 1 shows a typical table. Your first preference should be to sit at the seat labeled "Third base" (the reason for this will be explained later), but any seat will do. At any rate, I'll assume that you've found a table to your liking. Now it's time to dig into your wallet or purse and bring out the greenbacks. And let me emphasize that you will, indeed, be playing for money. In reality, you will be playing with the chips that your money has bought, but too many people forget that those red, green, and black chips represent authentic United States dollars; in many cases, hard-earned dollars.

On my first trip to Las Vegas, I was playing Blackjack

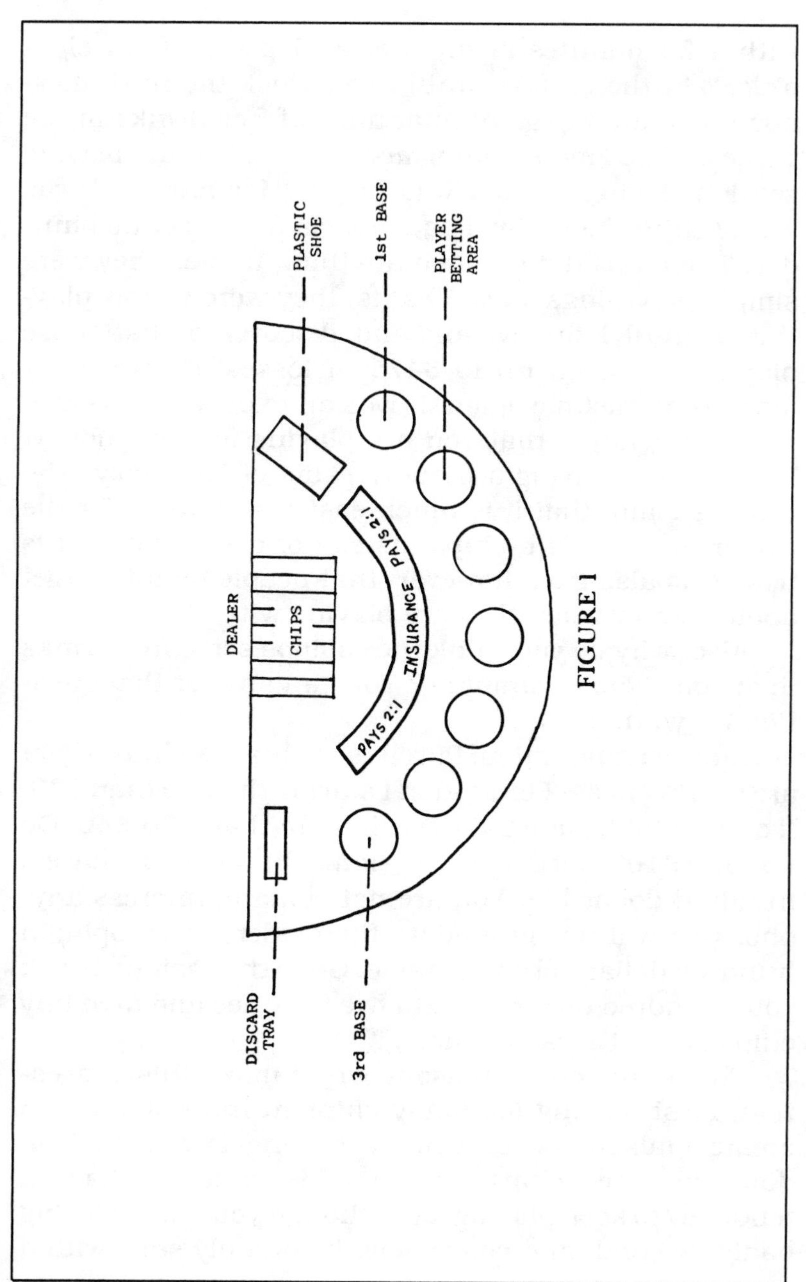
PLASTIC SHOE
1st BASE
PLAYER BETTING AREA
DEALER
CHIPS
PAYS 2:1
INSURANCE
PAYS 2:1
DISCARD TRAY
3rd BASE

FIGURE 1

within 35 minutes of my arrival. I played from eight o'clock in the evening until two o'clock the next afternoon, consuming great quantities of free drinks in the process. And I made a fatal mistake. During that playing session, I forgot that I was playing for money. I was losing chips. Mentally, I had made a fundamental blunder. The chips didn't mean anything to me. They were simply playthings; toys. That is, they were simply playthings until I finally quit and discovered that those playthings added up to $475 in losses! I have never made that mistake again. It was an expensive lesson.

Do not forget that you are playing for real money. You are *not* playing a friendly game of Monopoly. The casinos claim that it is much easier and faster for the dealer to work with chips instead of cash, and that is true. It is also true, however, that people tend to forget about money when they are playing with chips.

Also, why do you think the casinos serve free drinks to anyone who is gambling? You can answer that question for yourself.

Another suggestion: Purchase only a few chips. If you are playing at a $2 table, don't start with more than $20. If at a $5 table, don't start with more than $30-$40. Do not buy $100 worth of chips simply because you have a hundred dollar bill. You are not going to impress anyone; you will not intimidate the dealer by dropping a hundred dollar bill on the table. Go to the cashier, break your hundred dollar bill into five twenties and *then* buy chips at the Blackjack table.

There are several reasons why I make this suggestion. First, having too many chips in front of you can create a false sense of security; as long as you can look down and see chips on the table, you will have a tendency to keep playing, even though you may be losing badly. Second, and conversely, if you only start with a small amount, and those chips suddenly vanish, you will have an automatic alarm clock to help make you aware that you are, indeed, losing money. There will be times when you can sit at a table and do everything right, but still lose. The trick is to conserve your losses when you are losing. So, if that first $20 or $30 disappears, change tables! A new table can improve your morale and may help change your luck. In addition, your first time at the Blackjack tables will be an experiment of sorts. You're going to find out if you really understand the game, so don't make it an expensive training session.

To purchase chips, simply wait until the dealer is finished with the hand being played, place your $20 in front of or behind your playing spot, and "Change, please" or "Chips, please." Do not place the money *on* your playing (betting) area. This may lead the dealer to believe that you want to make a $20 cash bet. Some dealers will ask whether you want to bet that $20, others will go ahead and begin the deal. Don't leave any room for misunderstanding. Also, if the dealer does not give you the chips you want, tell her (I'll assume your dealer is female). If, for example, the dealer gives you four $5 chips and you only want to play for $2 a hand, push two of the chips back at her and request $1 chips.

Another point: The dealer can give you chips for your money, but the same is not true in reverse. She cannot buy back your chips when you leave the table. Chips can only be exchanged for money at the cashier's cage.

Okay, now you have your chips; probably two $5 chips and ten $1 chips. To make your initial wager, place the minimum bet in your playing area (see Figure 1). On some tables this area is rectangular; on others it is circular. Your chips should be stacked neatly, one on top of the other. When you see the dealer reminding people to stack their bets, it is not because she is a tidy person. It is because it is more difficult for a cheater to swindle the casino if the chips are stacked properly.

If you are making an odd wager, say $37, the chips should be stacked in the following manner: The largest-value chips on the bottom, the smallest-value on the top, and any others in the middle. If betting a green $25 chip, two red $5 chips, and two silver dollar tokens, the green would be on the bottom, the reds in the middle, the tokens on top. The casinos insist on this to help prevent cheating by the players. If this sounds a little strange, let me explain. Let's say you want to swindle the casino. You look at your first two cards, discover a total of twenty, and decide you have a very good chance of winning the hand. So, with lightning-fast fingers, you quickly add a few more chips to your bet while the dealer is concentrating on another player. Yes, I know that sounds silly. Who could possibly move that fast? No one could possibly get away with such a trick. Right? Wrong. Dealers and pit bosses tell me that people try to do it all the time. In our $37 example, with your chips stacked properly, you'd only be able to add a few dollars to the top of your bet, which would hardly be worth the effort. But, were the chips stacked so that the $25 chip was on top of the pile, you could easily add another $50 or $100, which *would* be worth the risk of getting caught. And that's why you must stack your chips properly.

What happens next depends on how many decks are in use at your table. There are single-deck tables, double-deck tables, four-deck tables, and even six-deck tables. Who knows? One day we might even see eight- or ten-deck tables. The more decks, the more benefit to the casinos. Personally, I prefer single- or double-deck tables. Other gamblers will disagree with me, but I believe that anyone who plays at a four- or six-deck table is deranged. Though it is possible to win with four or six decks, it is much more difficult than it is playing with one or two decks. If your hotel casino does not offer single or double decks, go somewhere else.

If you are in doubt as to how many decks are being used, ask the dealer. If there is a "shoe" (see Figure 1) on the table, at least four decks are being used. A "shoe" is a small plastic box which holds all the cards. Instead of dealing from her hands, the dealer slides the cards out of the shoe.

Now for the cards. It's a new shuffle. The dealer carefully mixes the cards, places them in front of your playing position, then stares at you as if she wants you to do something. Yes, that's right. She wants you to cut the cards. You comply, cutting the cards just as you do at home when you're playing bridge or poker. If you're playing at a two-, four-, or six-deck table, the dealer will pass you a small plastic card. That card is used to cut the deck. The dealer will extend all the decks so that you can insert the plastic card somewhere in the pile. The dealer then cuts the cards at that point.

After you've cut the cards, the dealer will discard the first one, two, or more cards into another small plastic tray to her right, called the "discard tray." This action is called "burning" a card. Later in this chapter I will explain its purpose.

The burning completed, the dealer starts dealing the cards from her left to her right, from first base to third base. In one- and two-deck games the player's cards are normally all dealt face down. In multiple-deck games the player's cards are often dealt face up. In either case, the dealer always has one card face up, one face down. The dealer's face-down card is called the "down" card or the "hole" card.

You watch your two cards slide toward you, pick

them up, and calculate the value of your hand. Don't be rushed. Take your time. Not all of us are mathematically inclined, so don't get nervous if the dealer gives you an annoyed look. Each card has a point value. Tens, Jacks, Queens and Kings are worth ten points each. Aces can be either one or eleven. All other cards are face value; a Six is worth six points, a Two is worth two points, and so forth.

The object of the game is to obtain a total of 21, or as close to 21 as possible, without exceeding 21. If you exceed a total of 21, you "bust" (lose automatically). If you do not bust, and your total is higher than the dealer's total, you win even money. For example, a $2 bet would win $3, a $10 bet would win $15, and so forth. A natural Blackjack is any two-card hand consisting of an Ace and any ten-value card. When you receive a natural, expose your cards immediately; turn them over and lay them down in front of your bet. If you don't immediately expose a natural, you may only be paid even money. Of course, if you're at a table where the cards are being dealt face up you needn't do anything but collect your winnings.

A natural Blackjack cannot lose, but it can be tied by a dealer natural. If the dealer's up card is a Ten or an Ace, she must peek at her hold card to see if she has a natural. If she does, everyone loses except the players who also have naturals. Those players tie, or push.

Anyway, you won your first hand. Congratulations. You are smiling joyously, so the dealer grins at you and then turns to the player at first base. That player is the first to choose from several available options. Since you were dealt a natural you don't need to exercise any options, but you still need to understand your alternatives. Here they are:

1) You can *stand* (or *stick*, or *stand pat*). This means that you are satisfied with your first two cards and don't want any more. To stand in a game where the cards are dealt face down, you simply slide your cards under the chips in your betting area. However, you *must not* actually touch the chips with your hands; the casino might think that you're cheating. If the cards are all dealt face up, simply wave your hand over the cards with your palm parallel to the table. You may also say, "I'm good," or "No more for me," or words to that effect.

2) You may request additional cards (or *hit*, or *draw*). This means that you are not happy with your first two cards and want to improve your total. If the cards were dealt face down, hold the cards in your hand and brush them lightly against the top of the table. The dealer will give you another card every time you make this motion. If the cards were all dealt face up, you can accomplish the same by brushing one of your index fingers on the table. Or you may say, "Hit me," or "give me another one," or words to that effect.

   If, by taking additional cards, you exceed a total of 21, you bust. In that case you must expose all your cards by laying them face up on the table. The dealer will then collect your cards and your losing wager.

   You can take as many additional cards as you want as long as you do not exceed 21. When you are through taking cards, you then stand as noted in #1 above.

3) You can *double down*. Explained later.

4) You can *split*. No, this doesn't you can grab your money and run for the exit, even though your initial two cards may inspire that reaction. I'll cover this one later, too.

5) You can *surrender*. Later.

6) You can buy *insurance*. Later.

As you watch the dealer move from player to player, you'll see your fellow gamblers exercising these options. When all the players have acted on their hands, it's the dealers' turn.

Ah, the poor dealer. While the players have several options, the dealer has only two:

1) If the dealer's total is 16 or less, she *must* take additional cards until she reaches 17-21 or busts.

2) If the dealer's total is 17 or more, she *may not* take additional cards.

After acting on her hand, the dealer then settles all wagers, usually working from third base back to first base. Then the next round begins. You place your bet, receive your cards, decide which option to exercise, and win or lose. See, I told you this was simple.

What makes Blackjack so interesting to play is that the gamblers have many options, the dealer only two. For the person who enjoys making quick decisions, no other casino game is as challenging or rewarding.

But how do you know when to exercise your options? Are there bad times to stand, good times to hit? And if you exercise your options properly, can you actually win? Yes, yes, and yes.

The following sections set forth the strategy you should use to win at Blackjack. You *must* study the charts, memorize and practice them if you are serious about winning. You cannot win by exercising your options with decisions based on intuition or lucky feelings. You *must* know the basic strategies in this book. They may seem difficult at first, so take your time. You can learn them!

HARD HOLDINGS

I don't know how the term originated, but it is quite descriptive. Often a hard holding of 12-16 puts you between a rock and a hard spot, creates a hard lump in your throat, or causes you to cast a very hard, disgusted look at the dealer.

A hard holding (also called *hard hand* or *stiff*) is a holding which can only be counted in one manner. A holding of Queen, Six can only be counted as 16. A holding of Eight, Seven can only be counted as 15. All hands are hard hands unless one or both of your cards is an Ace, since Aces can be one or eleven.

What do you do if you have a total of 15 and the dealer's up card is an Ace? What if the dealer is showing a Two or a Six? Sometimes the decisions are agonizing.

The chart which follows tells you what to do in every instance with hard holdings. Study it, memorize it, test yourself on it. Don't worry, you can learn it. I have tested this strategy in over a hundred thousand actual hands, plus used it in over a quarter million practice hands. It works.

There, that's not so difficult, is it? If you have 12 and the dealer is showing a Seven, you hit. If you have 12 and the dealer's up card is a Six, you stand. I give you an option on 16 versus a dealer Ten because this decision is never right, never wrong. If you have a total of 11 or less, hit. Stand on any total of 17 or more.

HARD HOLDING STRATEGY
S = STAND H = HIT * = OPTIONAL

THE DEALER IS SHOWING:	2	3	4	5	6	7	8	9	10	ACE
YOU HAVE										
4–11	H	H	H	H	H	H	H	H	H	H
12	H	H	S	S	S	H	H	H	H	H
13	S	S	S	S	S	H	H	H	H	H
14	S	S	S	S	S	H	H	H	H	H
15	S	S	S	S	S	H	H	H	H	H
16	S	S	S	S	S	H	H	H	*	H
17–21	S	S	S	S	S	S	S	S	S	S

FIGURE 2

But, you also ask, why do I hit when I'm holding 12 and the dealer is showing an Ace, stand when the dealer is showing a Six, hit when the dealer is showing a Two? Good questions, all. The answers lie in Figures 3 and 4 which follow.

The percentages in Figures 3 and 4 will vary as the game progresses, but not much. Consequently, they are the percentages to use in determining whether to hit or stand. It is these percentages, combined with the rigid rules governing the dealer's options, which give you the basic strategy set forth in Figure 2. When the dealer has a high chance of busting, you do not want to hit. In those cases, you play for the dealer to bust. You want to shift the risk from your hand to the dealer's hand.

For example: Assume that your hand is 15. The dealer is showing a Nine. Figure 4 indicates that you have a 53.8% chance of busting, should you hit. However, Figure 3 indicates that the dealer will finish with 17-21 77% of the time. If you stand on your 15, you will probably lose. Therefore, in this case, you take the offensive in an attempt to improve your hand.

DEALER IS SHOWING	% OF TIME DEALER WILL FINISH WITH 17 TO 21	% OF TIME DEALER WILL BUST
Ace	83%	17%
10	77%	23%
9	77%	23%
8	76%	24%
7	74%	26%
6	58%	42%
5	57%	43%
4	60%	40%
3	62%	38%
2	70%	30%

FIGURE 3

FIGURE 4

YOUR TOTAL IS	% OF TIME YOU CAN HIT WITHOUT BUSTING	% OF TIME A HIT WILL BUST YOU
11 or less	100.0%	00.0%
12	69.2%	30.8%
13	61.5%	38.5%
14	53.8%	46.2%
15	46.2%	53.8%
16	38.5%	61.5%
17	30.7%	69.3%
18	23.1%	76.9%
19	15.4%	84.6%
20	7.7%	92.3%

Now let's change the dealer's up card. Let's say she has a Five showing instead of a Nine. Figure 2 indicates that you should stand. The reasons are twofold: First, you have a 53.8% chance of busting if you hit. Second, the dealer has a 43% chance of busting. So why push your luck? Let the dealer risk busting *her* hand. You still may lose, but you've transferred the risk of busting to the dealer.

Similar examples can be drawn for all the other hard holding totals, but I'll let you figure them out for yourself. For those of you who are mathematically oriented and inquisitive, there is a list of reference material at the end of this book.

The basic strategy in Figure 2 does not change if your hand consists of more than two cards and you're playing against a shoe. If you have a three or four card total of 15, you should still hit against a dealer Nine. Assume you're playing against a shoe and you're dealt a Two and a Five. The dealer is showing a Queen. The basic strategy says to take a hit, so you do. You draw another Five, so now you've got a total of 12. The basic strategy says to hit a 12 against a dealer Queen; you do, and receive a Two, for a total of 14. Yes, I know you already have four cards, but that doesn't make any difference. Your lousy 14 will probably lose, so you must take another hit. You do, and receive an Ace. Now you have a 15 or 25, and since 25 is no good, you really have a hard 15. Now the sweat begins to trickle off your brow. The basic strategy says to hit a hard 15 when the dealer is showing any ten-value card. But you already have five cards, and you're convinced that if you take another hit you'll bust your hand. Your mind screams for you to stand pat. The other players are staring at you, waiting to see if you are stupid enough to draw a sixth card. It's decision time. And, since the basic strategy says to take a hit, you do so. Unfortunately, you receive a Ten and bust the hand, thereby losing your bet. Well, what can I say? You're not going to win every hand. The basic strategy is a guide which will help, but it will not miraculously cause you to win all the time. You might have caught a Six and won. That's why its called "gambling." Nothing ventured, nothing gained. However, in single and double deck games I prefer to stand on and three-card 15 or 16.

Whenever your are dealt an initial holding of 12, 13, 14, 15, or 16, your odds of winning are very slim. Again, that's why those totals are called hard holdings or stiffs. They are bad for your morale and bad for your pocketbook. Consequently, the strategy in Figure 2 is designed to make the best out of terrible situations.

As I stated earlier in this chapter, it is possible to do everything right and still lose. But if you use the basic strategy you will lose less than the other players at your table, who are relying solely on luck or whimsy. And I'm not discarding luck as being a valuable asset. What I'm saying is this: If you are using the basic strategy and you are still losing, you don't have any luck. Your karma is bad. Fate had decided to rob you of your money. You can't buck bad odds *and* bad luck. The basic strategy will help turn the odds in your favor and also protect you against the horrendous losses commonly associated with "bad luck." But if you sit down at a Blackjack table and continually receive 12's, 13's, 14's, 15's and 16's you are playing the wrong game. Leave the table and visit the hotel's steam room. If you use the basic strategy and still lose, you'll know fate is being unkind. If you *do not* use the basic strategy, there is no way to determine whether your losses are the result of bad luck or poor, foolish card play. On too many occasions to count, I have observed players making numerous ridiculous plays at the Blackjack tables, and then heard those same gamblers complain about not having any luck. Play wisely, and you can create your own luck.

Yes, you will win some of the time when you have hard holdings. Yes, it is even possible to win a majority of those hands. However, the odds are against you, overall. If, in fact, you are winning a majority of those hands, you may wish to increase your bets. You could be on a "hot streak," or the dealer could be on a "cold streak."

In the next sections you'll see that there are ways for you to make up for all those terrible hard holding hands, options which will mean money in your pocket if utilized properly. On the hard holding hands, you are really striving to break even. On the other hands you swing the odds in your favor.

DOUBLING DOWN

Perk up, your odds of winning are now improving. Pray that each new hand brings a double down opportunity. If you double down in the correct situations you can recapture the money you lost on all those miserable 15's and 16's. Here's your chance to get even with the dealer for giving you all those bad hands.

The term "doubling down" derives from two actions. First, you double your bet; second, you receive one additional card, normally dealt face down. Hence, you double down.

The rules governing doubling down vary from area to area. Most casinos allow you to double down on any two-card holding, others only on a holding of 10 or 11. It is to your advantage to play at casinos which allow you to double down on *any* two-card holding.

To double down, you expose your cards to the dealer, placing them face up in front of your betting area. Then you match your original bet with a like amount placed *adjacent* to your original bet. If your original wager was $5, you must extend another $5. If all the cards were dealt face up, simply match your original wager. The dealer will then give you one card. You do not have the option of taking more cards. You receive one card, and one card only. Sound risky? It *is* if you do it at the wrong times; it *is not* if you do it at the right times. The chart depicted in Figure 5 will tell you when the time is right.

You should double down on 11 against every dealer up card, on 10 against every dealer up card except a Ten or an Ace, on 9 only when the dealer is showing a Six or less. If you compare Figure 5 with Figure 3, you'll see how the doubling down strategy was developed. In essence, you want to double down whenever the dealer has a high probability of busting. Doubling on 11 against a dealer Seven, Eight, Nine, Ten, or Ace is an offensive attempt. Remember that in a deck of 52 cards there are sixteen ten-value cards (four tens, four Jacks, four Queens, and four Kings), so your chance of receiving a ten-value card on your double down is good. Also, you only want to double down on holdings which cannot be busted by the addition of one card; you would *not* double down on 12, 12, 14, or more.

I know one gambler who doubles down each time he has less than 12 and the dealer is showing a Five or a

FIGURE 5
DOUBLING DOWN
D = DOUBLE DOWN H = HIT

THE DEALER IS SHOWING:	2	3	4	5	6	7	8	9	10	ACE
YOU HAVE										
11	D	D	D	D	D	D	D	D	D	D
10	D	D	D	D	D	D	D	D	H	H
9	D	D	D	D	D	H	H	H	H	H

Six. Yes, I've seen him double down on a holding of 3. And, believe it or not, he wins more than he loses. However, when I tried the same strategy I was massacred. In any case, you don't want to be too greedy. Don't forget: When you double down you double your winnings, but you can also double your losses. Use doubling down wisely and you'll give yourself an edge over the casino.

SOFT HOLDINGS

A "soft" holding is any holding which can be counted in *more than one* manner. This can only happen when you have an Ace in your hand. Remember, an Ace can be counted as *either* one or eleven. If you have a holding of Ace, Five you have either 6 or 16. Since a holding of 16 is tantamount to certain death, you should count the Ace as one, for a total of 6.

If you have a holding of Ace, Nine, you will want to count the Ace as eleven, for a total of 20. You may also count it as one, for a total of 10, but why reduce a potential winning hand to an unknown?

Ace, Four could be 5 or 15. Ace, Seven could be 8 or 18. Obviously, having a soft holding gives you more flexibility. It is virtually impossible to bust a soft holding. But, ordinarily, a soft holding does not stay soft very long.

Assume you're dealt Ace, Five. You treat the Ace as a value of one, so your total is 6. You take a hit (you can't possibly bust) and catch a King. Your hand is no longer soft. Now you have a hard holding of 16(1+5+10).

Another example: You are dealt Ace, Three. You have either 4 or 14. You take a hit, and get a Two. Now you have Ace, Three, Two, which is worth either 6 or 16. You take another hit, an Eight. Ace, Three, Two, Eight totals

14. It *must* total 14. You have no other choice. If you treat your Ace as eleven, your total would be 11+3+2+8=24!

Soft holdings can make for very interesting hands. I am sure that this has happened to all seasoned Blackjack players, but I will relate this experience as an example. I was at a crowded casino on New Year's Eve, and all the two-deck tables were busy. I was possessed by gambling fever, so in a fit of stupidity, I decided to play at a four-deck table. On one hand, my initial two cards were Ace, Two. The dealer was showing a Ten. I took a hit. I received another Ace, giving me either 4(1+1+2) or 14(1+1+1+11+2). I then took another hit and received yet another Ace. Remember, I was at a four-deck table, so there were sixteen Aces in the shoe. Anyway, my six-card total was still only 7 or 17. I could have stopped at that point, but since the dealer was showing a ten, and since I could not possibly bust my hand with another hit, I brushed my cards on the felt and received a Five, which gave me a total of 12 (1+1+1+1+1+2+5). At that point, my soft holding finally became a hard holding. The interesting point is that my hand stayed soft for six cards which does not happen very often.

In case you're interested in whether I won or lost that hand, I suppose I should finish the story. I had to take two more hits to complete my hand. One was a Two, the other was a Five. My final hand was Ace, Ace, Ace, Ace, Ace, Two, Five, Two, Five for a total of 19. The dealer had 18. Horray for our side!

Figure 6 shows you what to do with various soft holdings against all dealer up cards. With soft holdings you really have three options: stand, hit, or double down.

When you read Figure 6 you'll see many doubling down opportunities. The reasons for doubling down a

SOFT HOLDINGS
S = STAND H = HIT D = DOUBLE DOWN

THE DEALER IS SHOWING:	2	3	4	5	6	7	8	9	10	ACE
YOU HAVE										
Ace,9	S	S	S	S	S	S	S	S	S	S
Ace,8	S	S	S	S	S	S	S	S	S	S
Ace,7	S	D	D	D	D	S	S	H	H	S
Ace,6	H	D	D	D	D	S	H	H	H	H
Ace,5	H	H	D	D	D	H	H	H	H	H
Ace,4	H	H	D	D	D	H	H	H	H	H
Ace,3	H	H	D	D	D	H	H	H	H	H
Ace,2	H	H	D	D	D	H	H	H	H	H

FIGURE 6

soft holding are threefold: First, you cannot possibly bust your hand. Second, in each of the situations depicted in figure 6 there is an excellent probability of the dealer busting. Finally, there is a good chance that you will receive a card which will improve your hand. So you have just enough of an edge to make it worthwhile to double your bet.

You always stand on Ace, Eight and Ace, Nine, because those hands are worth 19 and 20, respectively. You could double down on either of those hands against a dealer Five or Six, but again I caution you against becoming greedy. Explore this chart, study it, memorize it and compare it with Figure 3. You'll see that some of the situations call for defensive action, others for offensive action by the player. As with the chart for doubling down, astute use of soft holdings will increase your winnings.

SPLITTING

When you split your initial two cards you actually turn

one hand into two, with each treated as a separate hand which must be played. This can only happen when your first two cards are a pair. If your first two cards are Two, Two, you can split them. You can split Three, Three or Four, Four, or any pair including any two ten-value cards (Ten, Jack, Queen or King).

When you split your hand you must double your bet, since you will be playing two separate hands. The procedure is the same as that for doubling down; expose your cards to the dealer and match your bet with a like amount. If the cards were dealt face up, simply match your bet. But unlike doubling down, take care to create a space between your cards when you expose them. If you are splitting a pair and you lay them down so that one card is on top of the other, the dealer may think you want to double down. In any case, make sure the dealer understands that you want to split.

The dealer will deal a hit to the first card of your pair (the first of your two separate hands) and wait to see if you want additional cards on that hand. The hand is played like any other using the strategies that were discussed. You can hit or stand, and certain casinos will allow you to double down or resplit (see "Rule Variations," page 47). Once the first hand is completed, the dealer moves to your second hand.

There are rule variations for splitting, but one rule is the same at all casinos. If you split a pair of Aces, you will receive only *one* card, usually dealt face down, on each of your Aces. You have no options. You live or die with the single card that you are dealt on each Ace. In addition, should one or both of your Aces be dealt a ten-value card, you do not have a natural Blackjack. You simply have a total of 21 and are paid even money if you win. Remember, the only time you can have a natural Blackjack is on your initial two cards.

Here is the basic strategy for splitting.

SPLITTING PAIRS

S = STAND $ = SPLIT H = HIT D = DOUBLE DOWN

THE DEALER IS SHOWING:	2	3	4	5	6	7	8	9	10	ACE
YOU HAVE										
2,2	H	$	$	$	$	$	H	H	H	H
3,3	H	$	$	$	$	$	H	H	H	H
4,4	H	H	H	H	H	H	H	H	H	H
5,5	D	D	D	D	D	D	D	D	H	H
6,6	$	$	$	$	$	H	H	H	H	H
7,7	$	$	$	$	$	$	H	H	H	H
8,8	$	$	$	$	$	$	$	$	$	$
9,9	$	$	$	$	$	S	S	$	S	S
10,10	S	S	S	S	S	S	S	S	S	S
Ace,Ace	$	$	$	$	$	$	$	$	$	$

FIGURE 7

You should *always* split Ace, Ace and Eight, Eight. You should *never* split Ten, Ten or Five, Five. When holding Five, Five, you should use the rules for doubling down on Ten (see Figure 5). It is not a good idea to split Fours, but, if you feel lucky, you can split them against a dealer Five or Six.

You will note that at times you are taking the offensive, at other times the defensive. Holding Seven, Seven is no great joy. By splitting Sevens you may draw cards which will improve your chance of winning (nearly anything is better than 14). Splitting Nines is an offensive attempt when the dealer is showing a card worth less than a Six. Yet we do not split Nines against a dealer Seven for the simple reason that if the dealer has 17, you will beat her with your 18. Against a dealer Eight you should stand on Nine, Nine, hoping for a tie. Against a dealer Ten or Ace assume that your 18 will lose, so you split and try to save the bet by making at least one of the hands a winner. If one of the Nines draws a Two and A Ten you are in good shape even if you bust the other hand (you win one, lose one, and break even).

Splitting opportunities do not present themselves very often, but you should know how to handle them when they occur.

INSURANCE

This is one of the least understood of all the player options. Yet it can be quite beneficial one you know what buying insurance really means.

The only time you can buy insurance is when the dealer's up card is an Ace. In that case the dealer will ask all the players whether they want to buy insurance. If you want to buy insurance, place an amount equal to half your original wager into the area marked insurance (see Figure 1). The dealer then peeks at her hold card to see if she has a ten-value card for a natural Blackjack. If she does have a Blackjack, you lose your original wager (unless you also have a natural Blackjack), but you win two to one on your insurance bet. If the dealer does not have a Blackjack, you lose your insurance bet and the game continues in the normal manner, with each player then acting on their hands.

But you are *not* really buying insurance. In essence, you are simply making another bet. You are *betting* on whether or not the dealer has a natural Blackjack. And unless you are a card counter (explained later) this is a bad bet to make! Unless you are a card counter, there is only one possible instance when you *might* want to buy insurance — if you have a holding of 20. In that case, even if you lose the insurance bet, you stand a good chance of winning your original wager. If you had bet $5 you would lose $2.50 on the insurance bet but win $5 on the original wager, for a net gain of $2.50.

No matter what the dealers try to tell you, no matter what other players try to tell you, buying insurance is not a good bet unless you are a card counter. Some people will tell you that if you have a natural Blackjack as your holding you should always buy insurance if offered. Nonsense! Don't do it, again, unless you are a card counter.

SURRENDER

Yes, this player option is exactly what the word implies. You surrender your hand to the dealer. You give up. You wave a white flag over your head. And the result is that the dealer takes only *half* your bet. If you are a card counter this option can be very beneficial. If you are not a card counter this option may not be as great as it sounds.

To surrender your cards, simply turn them over and expose them to the dealer. If the cards were all dealt face up, simply say, "Surrender" or "I surrender." In either case, *do not* touch your bet. The dealer will take half your wager. The casino does not want you fooling around with your chips; they are always on guard for cheaters.

You may only exercise this option *before* acting on your hand. You cannot take a hit, bust, and then surrender. You must surrender your original two cards.

If you are not a card counter, there are only a few situations in which you *might* want to surrender. If your hand is 15 or 16 and the dealer is showing a ten-value card; or if your hand is a 14 made up of Seven, Seven and the dealer is showing a ten-value card. Otherwise, take your chances and try to beat the dealer.

Not all casinos offer this option, so always ask the dealer about surrendering.

CARD COUNTING

Card counting means counting certain cards in order to ascertain whether the deck is in favor of the players or the dealer. Yes, a deck of cards can fluctuate quite a bit in favor of one or the other. It has been proven by several people (see list of recommended reading) that the deck is favorable to the players when the ration of high cards remaining in the deck is grater than the ration of low cards. When the deck contains a high ration of low cards, ten-values and Aces, it's the player's turn to multiply his or her winnings.

If you are not a card counter, you may have even confused a favorable deck with "luck". Assume that you play at a six-deck table and that, by the time you begin to play, the majority of the low cards have already been played. You then win five hands in a row and decide that your luck is good. But, in fact, you won because the deck was favorable for the players. Of course, the reverse could also happen. You could sit down at a time when the deck is favorable for the dealer, lose five hands in a row, and decide that you have bad luck.

Card counting is not difficult. It *can* be very difficult if you use a complicated counting system, but exotic counting systems are best left to the experts. What you need is a system which is easy to use and easy to remember — a simple system which will help you win more and avoid losses. I will cover what I feel are the two easiest ways to count cards, and also a third, slightly more difficult option.

Counting Ten-Values

If you watch closely, whether the cards are dealt face up or face down, you will see every card that is played when players bust or when the dealer makes the settlements. All you must do is count the number of ten-value cards that you see. Will it help? Immensely! Is it worth the effort? Absolutely!

There are 52 cards in each deck, sixteen of which are ten-values. This means that approximately one of every three cards is a ten-value. If the deck is "even" (the ten-values are spread equally through the deck), one ten-value should be played for about every three cards. When only a few ten-values are dealt on a hand, the next round will be "rich" in ten-values. When a lot of ten-values are dealt on a hand, the next round should be "poor" in ten-values. If the deck is rich, the benefit is to the players. If the deck is poor, the benefit is to the dealer.

Common sense would tell us that, if the deck is rich in ten-values, the dealer has the same opportunity of being dealt a good hand as the players, and common sense would be correct. Just because the deck is rich in ten-values, you will not necessarily be dealt a pair of ten-values on the next hand. It might be the dealer who catches that pair of ten-values. So how does counting ten-values, knowing whether the deck is rich or poor, improve our winnings?

Example: The dealer is showing a ten-value. You have 11. The basic strategy says you should double down. However, from counting the ten-values, you know that the deck is very poor in ten-values. Should you still double down? Absolutely not!

Example: The dealer is showing a ten-value. You have a hard holding of 15. The basic strategy says to hit. But you know that the deck is very rich in ten-values. Should you still take a hit? No! You are almost certain to bust. Cross your fingers and hope the dealer doesn't have another ten-value for her hole card.

Example: The dealer shows an Ace, and asks if you want to buy insurance. You know that the deck was very rich in ten-values at the start of that round. Should you buy insurance? Of course.

Example: The dealer is showing a ten-value, a Nine, an Eight, or a Seven. You have a miserable 15. You know that the deck is rich in ten-values. Should you hit? Stand? No, you should do neither. This is a perfect example of when you should surrender, if you have that option.

Example: The dealer is showing a Five. You have a holding of 8. You know that the deck is rich in ten-values. Should you hit? No! Instead, you could double down. The dealer's chance of busting is even greater than normal, so take your best shot.

By counting ten-values, you can modify the basic strategies to greatly increase your advantage over the dealer, and dramatically increase your odds of winning.

Here's an easy way to count ten-values. I have found that, on the average, three cards are used by each player during each round. Some will play with their initial two cards, others will take multiple hits, but the average is usually three per player. That means that you should see, or count, one ten-value for each player, including the dealer, at your table on each round. And, by the way, I don't consider the deck to be rich or poor unless the ten-value count is at least three more or three less than what it should be.

Example: Six players plus the dealer. On the first hand of a new shuffle you count twelve ten-values. Is the deck rich or poor for the next round? Figure it out. Six players + the dealer = seven people. Seven ten-values should have been played; one for each player and one for the dealer. Since twelve were actually played, the remaining deck is very poor in ten-values.

Example: You are playing at a table with four other gamblers. For some undetermined reason, you are playing against a shoe of six decks. On the first round of cards you count three ten-values, on the second round you count only two ten-values, and on the third round you count six ten-values. Is the deck rich or poor in ten-values for the next round? Here's how to figure it out. You + four other gamblers + the dealer = a total of six people. So, approximately six ten-values should be played on each round. Three rounds of play should have seen eighteen ten-values. But how many did you count? Three + two + six = eleven. Consequently, the deck at that point is very rich in ten-values. Another benefit in knowing if the deck is rich or poor is that you can bet accordingly. If the deck is rich, to your advantage, you should increase your bet slightly. If the deck is poor, make a minimum wager.

Note: If there is too much fluctuation in your bets you will stand out to the casino personnel like the lone tree in a barren field. The casino will then either have the dealer reshuffle after every hand, effectively destroying your count, or even ask you to leave.

A good rule of thumb is that your maximum wager should not be more than three times your normal minimum bet. Some people recommend that your maximum bet should not exceed five times your normal wager, but I've found that if you suddenly increase your bet from, say, $10 to $50, you become a closely-watched gambler. Even worse, if you bet $10 again, it's obvious you're either a counter or sick of mind. If you win that $50 bet, you're a counter. If you lose it, you're sick of mind. So take my advice. If you normally bet $5 on each hand, your largest bet should be $15. If you normally bet $10 on each hand, your largest bet should be $30. Of course there are exceptions to this rule, such as when you are using a progressive betting system. But using a progressive betting system will not brand you as a counter.

If you are counting ten-values and you begin to gain confidence, here's a suggestion. I'll assume you are varying your bets from $5 to $15. Instead of wagering $5 when the deck is even(neither rich nor poor), bet $10. Then, when the deck is poor you can drop down to a $5 wager, when rich go up to $15. The reasons are twofold. First varying your bets by one unit up or down will not cause anyone to think you are a counter. Second, knowing the richness or poorness of the deck gives you enough additional knowledge to increase to $10, even if the deck is just even. Once you're comfortable with counting ten-values, you're a smarter player, so you can afford to wager a little more.

Counting ten-values is an easy way to help turn the odds in your favor, but it is not an exact science. However, knowing whether the deck is rich or poor gives you that extra bit of information which will add winnings to your gambling stake, or — and this is just as important — help protect you from unnecessary losses.

Just remember this: The deck can only be "rich," "poor," or "even." If it's even, you would continue to use the basic strategy outlined earlier in this chapter. If it is rich or poor, use your common sense. There are only a few minor adjustments that need to be made if the deck is rich or poor, and these have already been covered in the examples.

Counting Aces

This will not help as much as counting ten-values, but when the deck is rich in Aces you have an increased opportunity of being dealt a natural Blackjack. Also, when the deck is rich in Aces you have more opportunity of being dealt a soft holding, which gives you much more flexibility. And when the deck is rich in Aces, doubling down on a holding of 9 or 10 makes for an even greater chance for success.

In addition, if you can manage to count both Aces *and* ten-values, you could be one of the best informed players in the casino. Try it sometime; it's not that difficult. Or play with a friend. You can count the ten-values, your friend can count the Aces.

One in every thirteen cards should be an Ace. Start counting cards after you see an Ace. If more than thirteen cards are dealt without another Ace appearing, the deck is rich in Aces. The more cards dealt without an Ace appearing, the richer the deck will be in Aces. Conversely, if Aces appear more often than once in every thirteen cards, the deck is poor in Aces.

Every time the deck is rich in ten-values *and* Aces, people are invariably dealt natural Blackjacks. It never fails. So, whenever I note that the deck is rich in Aces and ten-values, I make my largest bet. You would be amazed at how many times I've been dealt a natural Blackjack with a maximum bet on the table. And don't forget, a natural Blackjack is paid off at three to two instead of even money.

Aces are powerful cards, even though few in number.

Listen closely the next time you play Blackjack. Sometime during your gambling session, one of your fellow gamblers will receive a natural Blackjack, moan, and then say something like this: "Damn it, I never have a big bet on the table when I catch a Blackjack. Seems like I always get them when I bet small."

Well, no kidding.

But *you*, since you will be watching those precious Aces, will be prepared for those natural Blackjacks.

Positives and Negatives

For those of you who are willing to devote some time to serious card counting, here's your system. If you can master it, you'll be one of the toughest, hardest-to-beat Blackjack players in any casino. But let me warn you: It takes a *lot* of practice.

This system can be worked with infinite variations, so I'll explain the way I use it. And, by the way, I only use this system when I'm playing against a shoe. If I'm playing against one or two decks, I simply count ten-values and Aces. Not that counting ten-values and Aces is better, it's just less mentally demanding and fatiguing.

Count ever ten-value card as worth minus one, or negative one (-1). Count all Aces as worth negative two (-2). Assign all Threes, Fours, Fives and Sixes a value of positive one (+1). Do not bother to count Twos, Sevens, Eights, or Nines. The object is to keep a running total as all the cards are played. If the running total is negative, the deck is in favor of the dealer. If the running total is positive, the deck is in favor of the players.

Think about it for a moment, and it will start to make sense. If the count is a positive number, a lot of low-value cards have been played, which then means the rest of the deck has a lot of high-value cards remaining in it. And you, as a player, want to be aware of situations when the deck is made up of a high ratio of high-value cards.

Try a few examples. The following cards are played: Ace, Three, Two, King. What's the count? The Ace is worth minus two (-2). The Three is worth positive one (+1). The Two has no value assigned to it, so don't count it. The King is worth minus one (-1). So what you have is, (-1)+(+1)+(-1). Added together, the count becomes a total of minus two (-2), which tells us that of the cards played so far, more high-value cards have been played than low-value cards.

Another example. These cards are played: Jack, Four, Five, Seven, Eight, Three, King. What's the running count? This time add the totals just as you would in a real game. The Jack is a minus one (-1), so your beginning total is minus one(-1). The Four is a positive one (+1), so now the total is zero (0). The Five is a positive one (+1), so your total becomes positive one (+1). The Seven and the Eight do not count. The Three is a positive one (+1), so your total adds to positive two (+2). The King is a negative one (-1), which brings the running total back down to positive one (+1). In this example, your running total of positive one (+1) tells you that of all the cards played thus far, more low-value cards have been played than high-value cards.

Again, a positive running total tells you that the deck is composed of a favorable ration of high-value cards. Positive means good, negative means bad for the players. The more often you have a positive running total, the more often you will win.

Now here's how to adjust your play based on this running total. I've found that the total must reach at least positive four (+4) or negative five (-5) before I make any changes in my bets or in the basic strategy. When that happens, here's what to do:

1) With a running count of plus four (+4) or plus five (+5), double your wager. If you've been betting $5, bet $10.

2) With a running count of plus six (+6) or more, triple your bet. If you've been wagering $5, wager $15.

3) With a running count of plus five (+5) or more:

   a) Double your bet — but only after a winning hand. If you bet $15, make your next bet $30. This will not indicate that you are counting cards, for the simple reason that gamblers often double up after a win.

   b) Always buy insurance if offered.

   c) Double down on all totals of 8 against all dealer Fours, Fives, And Sixes.

   d) Do not hit any hard holdings of 15 or 16.

   e) Surrender any hard holdings of 14, 15 or 16 against a dealer ten-value.

4) With a running count of minus five (-5), minus six (-6), or less:

   a) Do not double down on a holding of 11 unless the dealer is showing a Five or a Six.

   b) Do not double down on a holding of 10 unless the dealer is showing a Five or a Six.

   c) Do not split Aces unless the dealer is showing a Five or a Six.

   d) Never surrender any hand, regardless of how bad it seems.

The list could go on and on, but common sense should prevail. All these rules mean additional winnings or reduced losses, so try to remember them when you are using the Negative-Positive counting system. It is the most troublesome system to learn, but it is also the most accurate.

I should now explain two statements which I made earlier in this chapter. First, I indicated that, if at all possible, you should sit at third base. The reason for choosing that position is that by sitting at third base you are able to see, and therefore count, more cards before you need to exercise any options on your hand. This is beneficial even if you're not a card counter, but it is especially beneficial if you have a card counting system. The more cards you can count, and the more accurate your count, the more you turn the odds in your favor.

Example: At the start of a round of play, you note that the deck is "rich" in high-value cards. Consequently, you know that the remaining portion of the deck should be favorable for the players. You are dealt a Seven and a Four. The dealer is showing a Queen. Since the remaining deck is composed of a high ration of high-value cards, you anticipate doubling down. But you are seated at third base, and the five or six players acting before you all take hits. They all receive ten-value cards. Would you still double down? Probably not. By the time it's your turn to exercise your options, the deck is no longer "rich" in high-value cards.

Your second choice of places to sit should be at first base. The reason? At first base, you are able to exercise your options before all the other players. In the example stated above, had you been seated at first base, you would definitely have doubled down. Had you been at first base, the other players would not have depleted the high ratio of high-value cards remaining in the deck.

Now that I've told you why you should sit at first or third base, let me try to confuse. you. Most card counters that I've met prefer first or third base. Most pit bosses know that most card counters prefer third or first base. Consequently people who sit at third or first base tend to be watched more closely by the pit bosses, especially if the players in those two positions are wining consistently or varying their bets. So, while third and first base seats are preferable, don't feel cheated if you can't find one. In fact, there is nothing wrong with sitting in one of the middle seating positions. From the middle of the table it is actually easier to count cards, for the simple reason that you are midway between third and first bases and you therefore can see all the cards with less difficulty. And now that you may be confused as to where you should sit, let me make one last statement: If you are a card counter, you should try to sit at third or first base. If you are a beginning card counter, if you are not adept at camouflaging your counting, or if you are not an expert, do not sit at third or first base.

I also mentioned earlier that dealers will "burn" one or more cards from the top of the deck or decks before beginning each new deal. Now that we're talking about card counting, I can tell you the reason the top card (or cards) is "burned" is to make life more troublesome for card counters. When counting cards, it is imperative to see as many cards as possible. If the dealer burns the top four cards, and all four cards are ten-values, your count will never be entirely accurate. The more cards the casino burns, the more difficult it is to count cards.

I once played at a casino where the dealer burned the top eight cards from a four-deck shoe. I thought she had made a mistake, so I asked her if burning eight cards was a new policy at that casino. Her answer was, "Sometimes." Needless to say, I left that casino after a few hands. But before I exited, I noted that a lady sitting at third base was obviously a card counter. Unfortunately, she was making plays that no person in their right mind would ever make, such as doubling down on a total of 7, and winning. So it became apparent that the dealer had burned eight cards in an attempt to discourage the counter.

While I'm thinking of it, here's another point I'd like to make. To my way of thinking, the players are all in a war against the dealer. No, that doesn't mean we should hate all dealers. To the extent that we players are all trying to win, it makes sense that we should help one another as much as possible. Therefore, if the cards are dealt face down, don't be afraid to let the players on either side of you see your cards. I am a card counter. So when the people around me try to conceal their cards so I can't see them, I sometimes become perturbed. The more cards I can see, the better my count, and the greater my chance of winning. Conversely, I always let the people around me see my cards, in the hope that a small amount of additional knowledge may help them. If I have a holding of 11 and everybody around me has two ten-value cards in their hand, I will certainly think twice before doubling down. Don't hide your cards from the other players!

MONEY MANAGEMENT

By this point, you should know the basic strategies and have an idea on how to count cards. Now let me make a statement: None of that means *anything*, unless you manage your money properly. You can play like a genius and still leave Las Vegas or Atlantic City with horrendous losses if you don't use your money with the utmost care and diligence.

My suggestion is this: Don't bother sitting down to play unless you have at least fifty units. A unit could be $2 or $5 or $100, but, whatever it is, you should have fifty. If your unit is $2, fifty units would be $100. If your unit is $5 you should have $250. You must have at least fifty units to protect yourself against extended losing streaks, which *do* occur no matter how well you play.

Next, you *must* change tables if you lose five units. There are times when the composition of the deck is such that it favors the dealer for long stretches. This can be true whether you are playing with one deck, two decks, or multiple decks. Again, what some of you may think is "bad" luck can actually be caused by the composition of the cards. If the majority of the high value cards are situated in the last half of the deck or decks, which is quite possible, then the first half of the deck or decks will greatly favor the dealer.

If you're playing with six decks, there are 312 total cards in the shoe, minus a few burn cards. Approximately half the decks, about 156 cards, will be played before the dealer reshuffles. If you are playing with four other gamblers, you could complete from eight to thirteen rounds of play before the deck is reshuffled. Therefore, if the composition of the decks is unfavorable, you could lose from eight to thirteen or more units, even if you play each and perfectly. And it is also possible for the decks to contain the same composition for several hours at a time; that is, the decks could remain unfavorable for the players for long stretches of time. Why play against a dealer who is beating your brains out? I don't care if you need to change tables every five minutes...keep changing until you stop losing, keep changing until you find a table where the composition of the decks is more favorable.

Also, if you win as many as ten units at any table, *do not* lose it back! As soon as you start winning, put your original chips in your pocket and play with your winnings. Once you've won ten units, do not allow yourself to slip backwards. Leave the table before the casino can recapture its losses.

Lastly, if you win as many as twenty-five units, change your unit. If your unit was $2, for example, change it to $5. When you are winning, you must push for all you can. The player most feared by the casinos is the player who gradually increases his or her bets for maximum profits. If you increase your unit and start losing, go back to your original unit. If you win another fifteen units, increase your unit again. But one word of caution: If you are a $2 bettor and increasing your unit to $5 or $10 makes you nervous, stay with a lower unit. I know people who play faultlessly with $5 bets, but lose control if they increase to $25 or $25 bets.

RULE VARIATIONS

Not all casinos use the same rules governing the player and dealer options. What follows is a list of the differences which you may find. Remember to ask about the rules *before* you start playing.

1) *Doubling down*: In Las Vegas and Atlantic City the player can double down on any initial two-card holding. In Reno and Lake Tahoe the player may *only* double down on holdings of 10 or 11, which limits double down opportunities and is subsequently a disadvantage for the player.

2) *Splitting*: In Las Vegas, Reno, and Lake Tahoe pairs may be split and resplit, Aces receive only one hit. In Atlantic City, pairs may be split but not resplit.

3) *Surrender:* This is an optional rule in Nevada, so ask everywhere you play. Until late 1981, the player could use surrender at all casinos in Atlantic City. However, the casino owners

convinced the Gambling Commission that the surrender option was going to cause them financial ruin. Consequently, you can no longer use the surrender option in Atlantic City.

4) *Doubling down after splitting*: Assume that you split a pair of Sixes and then receive a Five on the first Six. In Nevada, at only a handful of casinos, you may then double down on your 11. This is very beneficial to the player, so seek out casinos which offer this option. This option is available at all Atlantic City casinos.

5) *Dealer options*: In some casinos the dealer *must* stand on any 17. In others the dealer *may* stand on a soft 17 (Ace, Six). In still others, the dealer *must* hit a soft 17. It is to your advantage to play *only* where the dealer *must* stand on all 17's, whether soft or hard.

6) *Dealer Blackjacks*: In Atlantic City, all Blackjack games are dealt from a shoe of four or six decks. If the dealer shows a ten-value or an Ace, she *cannot* peek at her hold card until *after* all the players have acted on their hands. This is to prevent collusion between dealers and players. If a player splits or doubles down, only to find out that the dealer has a natural Blackjack, the player loses *only* the original wager, which is neither an advantage or a disadvantage. Check to see if your casino offers this option.

7) *Double exposure*: In some Nevada casinos both the dealer's cards are dealt face up. This, of course, gives the player a tremendous advan-

tage as it eliminates any speculation abut the dealer's hole card. If the dealer is showing a total of 20, for example, you would hit your total of 19. But what the casinos give you with the right hand, they take back with the left. Here's what I mean. Though you have the advantage of seeing the dealer's hole card, in this game you are only paid even money if you receive a natural Blackjack. And some casinos count all ties or pushes in this game as losses for the player. Only a fool would play against such heavy odds.

If you haven't tried double-exposure Blackjack yet, you might want to try it at a one-dollar or two-dollar table, using your "fun" money. And make sure you know *all* the rules before you start making bets.

That's all for this chapter, but don't forget to read and study the practical advice in the last chapter of this book, which covers all the casino games. And even if you're not interested in Craps, Roulette, Baccarat, Slot Machines or Keno, read the other chapters, anyway. Who knows? You may want to play one of those games some day.

2

CRAPS

THIS GAME INTIMIDATES many people. You see enthusiastic gamblers clustered around a large table with chips of all colors being thrown, shifted, placed and removed with alarming speed. The money changes hands so fast that it is puzzling for the novice, and there are so many betting options that most people don't have the foggiest notion what is happening. Pass, Don't Pass, Come, Don't Come, Hard Eight, Wrong Bettors, Right Bettors, Buying numbers, Placing numbers, laying the odds, taking the odds, Any Craps, Hardway bets; is it any wonder why so many know so little about this game?

If the dice are "hot," you can win or lose a fortune in a matter of minutes, depending on how you are betting. But before you rush to the first Crap table you see, a firm understanding of the game is necessary. For, unlike in Blackjack, in Craps it is impossible to obtain an edge

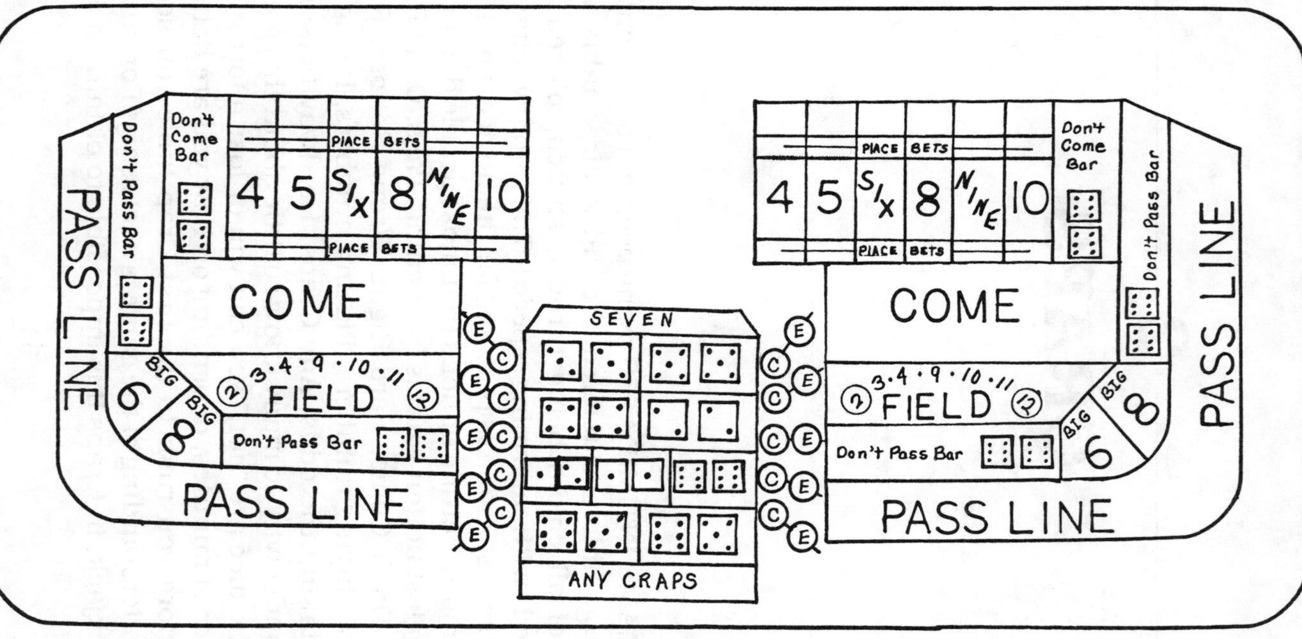
DEALER
BOXMAN
DEALER
PASS LINE
Don't Pass Bar
Don't Come Bar
PLACE BETS
4
5
SIX
8
NINE
10
PLACE BETS
COME
2
3·4·9·10·11
12
FIELD
BIG
6
BIG
8
Don't Pass Bar
PASS LINE
SEVEN
ANY CRAPS
C
E
PLACE BETS
4
5
SIX
8
NINE
10
PLACE BETS
Don't Come Bar
Don't Pass Bar
PASS LINE
COME
2
3·4·9·10·11
12
FIELD
BIG
8
BIG
6
Don't Pass Bar
PASS LINE
STICKMAN

FIGURE 1

over the casino. No matter what bet you make, the casino will have the advantage. However, that advantage is very small on some of the bets.

The game is played on a large table normally covered with green felt, with each betting option clearly marked by yellow or white lettering and boundaries (see Figure 1). The layout will vary from casino to casino, but, once you familiarize yourself with one layout, all are quite easy to understand.

Two dealers, a stickman, and a boxman supervise the action. The dealers settle the bets, assist the players in making proper wagers and, in general, do an incredible job of keeping track of the action. The stickman assists the dealers, controls both the dice and the center table bets, and keeps up a constant chatter to enliven the game. The two dealers and the stickman rotate their positions, each working the stick and both sides of the table. The boxman is the person sitting behind the table who looks like he is guarding the casino's chips; one of his responsibilities *is* to control the casino's money. In addition, the boxman watches the game to ensure proper payoffs, keeps a sharp eye on the dice, and is constantly on guard for cheats or collusion between dealers and players.

Two dice are used, each with six sides marked with from one to six small dots. When the two dice are rolled, there are 36 possible outcomes (totals of two dice). Before you can understand the various bets and your chances for success, you *must* understand how each number can be rolled. Study Figure 2 until you *fully* understand it.

Please note that Seven can be rolled in six combinations. Six and Eight can each be rolled in five ways. Five and Nine can be rolled in four ways. Four and Ten can each be rolled in only three ways, Three and Eleven in

OUTCOME	CAN BE ROLLED IN THESE COMBINATIONS OF TWO DICE
2	(1,1)
3	(1,2) (2,1)
4	(1,3) (2,2) (3,1)
5	(1,4) (2,3) (3,2) (4,1)
6	(1,5) (2,4) (3,3) (4,2) (5,1)
7	(1,6) (2,5) (3,4) (4,3) (5,2) (6,1)
8	(2,6) (3,5) (4,4) (5,3) (6,2)
9	(3,6) (4,5) (5,4) (6,3)
10	(4,6) (5,5) (6,4)
11	(5,6) (6,5)
12	(6,6)

FIGURE 2

only two ways. Two and Twelve can only be rolled in one way each. The chance of any of those numbers being rolled on any given throw of the dice is depicted in Figure 3.

In order for you to comprehend the various bets and why they work the way they do, it is essential that you understand Figures 2 and 3. But before I describe all the betting options, let me cover the basic procedures of

FIGURE 3

NUMBER	CHANCE OF BEING ROLLED
2 or 12	1 out of 36, or 2.8%
3 or 11	2 out of 36, or 5.6%
4 or 10	3 out of 36, or 8.3%
5 or 9	4 out of 36, or 11.1%
6 or 8	5 out of 36, or 13.9%
7	6 out of 36, or 16.7%

play. As I did with Blackjack, I will assume that you are approaching a Crap table for the first time.

Strolling through the casino early one morning, you see a Crap table being opened. No one is playing there yet, so you decide this is an opportune time to finally master this game. You station yourself next to the stickman and purchase chips from the dealer on your end of the table. You're hoping that no one else tries to play at the table so you can learn the game slowly, but, before you can ask the dealers what you're supposed to do, eighteen other gamblers swarm around the table. Suddenly, all hell breaks loose. Players start throwing chips all over the layout, issuing instructions to the dealers like, "Eight the hard way!," "Any Craps!," "Place the numbers!", "Gimme the Big Six!," etc. The stickman suggests, "Cover the field!," or "Bet the line!" Then he calls, "New shooter comin' out!" and looks at you as if you're supposed to do something as he pushes six or more dice in front of you. You sense a slight tingling in your stomach, feel foolish for a moment, and almost decide to leave the table because you don't have any idea of what's happening. At least that's what happened to *me* the first time I played Craps.

Here's what you do: First you must place a bet. It can be either on the Pass Line or the Don't Pass, but you must make a bet before you can throw the dice. If you don't care to roll the little cubes, simply tell the stickman and he'll pass the dice to the first person on your left. If you're not going to roll the dice, you needn't place a bet. But, for this example, I'll assume that you want to roll the dice. Next, you select two of the dice that the stickman has pushed in front of you. It doesn't make any difference which two you pick out. If you want to look like an experienced shooter (person rolling the dice), hold the dice in your hands for a moment, shake them, blow on them, and give them directions as to what outcome you'd like, eg. "Come on, Seven!"

Okay, now you have the two dice in your hands. Your next step is to throw them hard enough that they travel the distance of the table and hit the far end of the table. This is important. If you don't hit the far end of the table on your first throw, the stickman will probably tell you to do so on your next. This is because the casino wants a "true" roll, which can only be accomplished when the dice bounce off the padded end wall of the table. Knowing this, you now heave the dice so hard that they fly over the end of the table, strike a pit boss in the face, and skitter across the floor. If this happens, don't fret. The stickman will simply pass you more dice and let you start over again.

After a Point is established, you may need to roll the dice many times before obtaining either the Point or a Seven. During all those rolls, chips will be flying, people will be screaming their ecstasy or dread, and it may seem as though mass confusion reigns. Do not be concerned. Simply keep rolling the dice until the stickman pushes them in front of someone else. And, above all, do not hesitate to ask the dealer any questions which pop into your beleaguered mind. The dealers are there to help!

You continue to roll either Come-out rolls or Point rolls until you lose your bet. The dice are then passed clockwise around the table to the next shooter. You may then either leave the table or make additional bets. It is up to you.

In the following sections a short description is given of each bet available in Craps. If you don't understand the bet after your first reading, don't feel stupid. *Keep reading until you do understand*!! After several readings, you will find that there is no great mystique to this game, and, once you understand the bets, this is an easy game to play.

PASS LINE

Please note in Figure 1 that this bet covers a large portion of the Craps layout. This is one of the most popular bets and one of the easiest to understand.

A Pass Line bet should be made *only* before a Come-out roll. That's important to remember. If you approach a table and do not know whether the shooter is making Come-out or Point rolls, look for a large white disc which will be placed on one of the numbers Four, Five, Six, Eight, Nine, or Ten on the layout. If the disc is on any of those numbers, the next roll is *not* a Come-out roll. The disc indicates a Point has already been established and any subsequent rolls will be Point rolls. So, if the white disc is on one of the numbers, you must wait to make a Pass Line bet until the shooter either makes the Point or passes the dice to the next shooter.

To make this wager, simply place your chips anywhere within the Pass Line boundaries. Your wager will be won or lost in the following manner:

1) If the shooter throws a Seven or Eleven on the come-out roll, you win. The payoff is even money; for example, a $5 bet wins $5.

2) If the shooter throws a Two, a Three, or a Twelve on the Come-out roll, you lose.

3) If the shooter throws a Four, a Five, a Six, an Eight, A Nine, or a Ten on the Come-out roll, you have a Point. Then, if the shooter rolls your Point *before* rolling a Seven, you win even money. If the shooter rolls a Seven before rolling your Point, you lose.

Example: The Come-out roll is an Eight. Your bet remains on the Pass Line. The shooter then rolls a Four, a Three, an Eleven, a Nine, a Six, and another Six. None of those rolls have any effect on your bet! Only Seven or Eight (the Point) can make you a winner or loser. The shooter then throws a Three, a Two, an Eleven, and an Eight. Congratulations. You just won because the shooter rolled your Point (Eight) before rolling a Seven.

When betting the Pass Line you are essentially wagering on the shooter, betting that the shooter will either throw a Seven or an Eleven on the Come-out or make the Point. People who bet on the shooter are termed "Right" Bettors.

To analyze this wager, or any others, refer to Figures 2 and 3. Seven can be rolled in six ways, Eleven can be rolled in two ways; Two, Three, and Twelve can be rolled in a total of four ways. On the Come-out, eight combinations (outcomes) can win for you, and four will cause a loss; consequently, the odds are in your favor on the Come-out.

However, if a Point is established, you lose the advantage. Regardless of what Point is established, there is a greater chance of Seven being rolled than any other number.

To summarize, on the Come-out roll you have a 22.2% chance of winning, an 11.1% chance of losing. After a Point is established you have an 8 - 14% chance of winning, a 16.7% chance of losing.

Note: For the rest of the betting options, I'll let you figure out your chances of winning and losing for yourself, using the same procedure used here. Figures 2 and 3 contain all the information you need to do this.

DON'T PASS

With one slight exception, this bet is the exact opposite of a Pass Line bet. The rules governing winning or losing are reversed, for now you are betting *against* the shooter. People who bet against the shooter are termed "Wrong" Bettors.

This wager can be made only *before* a Come-out roll. Place your chips in the Don't Pass section of the layout and wait for the dice to determine your fate.

1) If the shooter throws a Seven or an Eleven on the Come-out, you lose.
2) If the shooter throws a Two or a Three on the Come-out, you win even money; for example, $5 wagered wins $5.
3) Here's the small twist. Note, in Figure 1 the Bar Twelve symbols in the Don't Pass section. If the shooter throws a Twelve on the Come-out, you tie. On some tables, a roll of either Two or Three may tie instead of Twelve, but on most tables Twelve ties. In any case, the symbols in the Don't Pass section of the layout will tell you which number ties.
4) If the shooter throws a Four, a five, A Six, an Eight, A Nine, or a Ten, you have a Point. If the shooter rolls the Point before a Seven, you lose. Should the shooter roll a Seven before the Point, you win even money.

COME BET

On the Come-out roll your chance for success is only 8.3%, your chance of losing 22.2%. But, if a Point is established, your chance of winning improves to 16.7%, your chance of losing drops to 8-14%, giving you the advantage. This wager, with one exception, is *identical* to a Pass Line bet. The lone difference is that a Pass Line bet is made *before* a Come-out roll, while a Come bet is made only *after* a Come-out roll. If a Point has already been established when you arrive at the Crap table, and you don't want to wait for the next Come-out roll, you can make a Come bet. Again, you are betting on the shooter. Place your chips in the Come area of the layout and wait for the next throw of the dice.

1) If the shooter's *very next* roll is Seven or Eleven, you win even money.

2) If the shooter's *very next* roll is Two, Three, or Twelve, you lose.

3) Any other outcome establishes a Point for your Come bet.

   Note: The Point for your Come bet may be different from the Point established on the original Come-out.

   Example: I'll start at the beginning. On the Come-out roll the shooter throws a Six, so Six is the Point for the Pass Line bets. Now you approach the table and bet Come. The shooter's very next roll is an Eight, so Eight is the Point for your Come bet. Had the shooter rolled another Six, the Six would have been the Point for your Come bet. But don't let all these numbers confuse you. Point is determined by the first roll of the dice after you make your Come bet. That's all you must remember. In fact, you don't even have to remember it. As soon as the Point is established for your Come bet the dealer will move your chips from the Come section to your Point number. Just watch your money. At any rate, if a Point is established for your Come bet:

4) You win even money if the shooter rolls your Come Point before a Seven. If the shooter rolls a Seven first, you lose.

The percentages for winning or losing a Come bet are exactly the same as for a Pass Line bet.

DON'T COME

That's right, a Don't Come bet is nearly the exact opposite of a Come bet. A Don't Come bet is also exactly the same as a Don't Pass bet, with one exception; a Don't Pass bet can be made only *before* a Come-out roll, while a Don't Come bet can be made only *after* a Come-out roll. You are betting against the shooter.

Place your chips in the Don't Come section, then win or lose in the following manner:

1) If the shooter throws a Seven or an Eleven on the very next roll, you lose.

2) If the shooter throws a Two or a Three on the very next roll, you win even money.

3) Here's the same twist as with the Don't Pass wager. If the shooter rolls a Twelve, you tie.

4) Any other outcome is your Don't Come Point. If a Seven is then rolled before your Don't Come Point, you win even money. If the Don't Come Point is rolled first, you lose.

As soon as the Point for your Don't Come bet is established, the dealer will move your chips from the Don't Come section to the box just above your Don't Come Point. Again, watch your money. There may be several bets in that little box, and you want to make sure you know which is yours.

The percentages for this wager are identical to those for a Don't Pass bet.

Now I'll recap the first four bets in case you're confused. Pass Line and Come bets are won and lost in exactly the same manner. The only difference between the two is that a Come bet can be made only *after* a Come-out roll, while a Pass Line bet should be made only *before a Come-out roll.*

Don't Pass and Don't Come bets are won and lost in exactly the same manner. The only difference between the two is that a Don't Come wager can be made only *after* a Come-out roll, while a Don't Pass bet can be made only *before* a Come-out roll.

With only these four options, you can play Craps all day. If shooters are making numerous passes (rolling Sevens or Elevens on the Come-out, or making their Points) you should bet Pass or Come. When shooters are not making passes, you should bet Don't Pass or Don't Come. All four of these wagers are even money payoffs, all have the same overall advantage for the casino, approximately 1.4%. As far as the casino's advantage is concerned, these four bets are the best ones for the player.

ODDS BETS (ALSO CALLED "FREE ODDS")

When you bet Pass Line, Don't Pass, Come or Don't Come, you are allowed to make a corresponding Odds bet if the shooter establishes a Point. With Pass Line and Come, you are *taking* the odds on the shooter making the Point. With Don't Pass and Don't Come you are *laying* the odds against the shooter making the Point. These odds are also called Free Odds because the payoffs are exactly correct; the casino holds no advantage over the player.

If you study Figure 1 you will not find an area in which to make Odds bets for the very simple reason that there is none. Because of this fact, many players are not aware that these bets are available. By taking or laying these odds the player reduces the casino's advantage on Pass Line, don't Pass, Come, and Don't Come from 1.4% to .8%. Of course, this is quite possibly the reason these bets are not advertised on the layout.

These are excellent bets for the player. You run the risk of losing faster because of the additional wager, but you can also increase your winnings. I'll take them one at a time.

PASS LINE ODDS BET

First you must make a wager on the Pass Line. Then, if a Point is rolled, you can back up you Pass Line bet by taking the odds on the Point. The exact amount of this wager depends on the casino's guidelines, but you can normally bet at least as much as your original wager on the Pass Line. To make this bet, place your additional chips an inch or two behind your original pass Line bet. Both your Pass Line bet and the Odds bet then lose if a Seven is rolled before the point, win if the Point is rolled before a Seven. The Pass Line bet still pays even money, but the associated Odds bet pays in the following manner:

1) If the Point is Four or Ten, you are paid two to one. A bet of $5 would pay you $10.
2) If the Point is Five or Nine, you are paid three to two. A wager of $10 would pay you $15.

3) If the Point is Six or Eight, you are paid six to five. A wager of $5 would pay you $6.

Because of these payoffs, you must take care to always wager the correct amount to receive the correct payoffs. When in doubt, ask the dealer. Note that an Odds bet of $5 four the Four, ten, Six or Eight could be paid correctly, but a $5 bet on Five or Nine would produce an uneven payoff ($7.50). On uneven payoffs the casino will round down to the next lowest even payoff. A $5 bet on Five or Nine would only pay $7. This is because the lowest value chip used by the casino is worth $1. They will not give change of fifty cents or twenty-five cents. Therefore, a bet on five or Nine must be made in Multiples of $2; a bet on six or Eight must be made in multiples of $5.

Example: You bet $10 on the Pass Line. The shooter rolls an Eight, which becomes your Point. You then place an additional $10 an inch or so behind your Pass Line wager. The shooter then throws a Four, a Five, a Six, a Nine, an Eleven, another Eleven, a Two, and a Three. None of those numbers mean anything to you. The only outcomes which affect your bets are Seven and Eight. If Seven is rolled before Eight, you lose both the Pass Line bet and the Odds bet. If Eight is rolled before Seven, you win both the Pass Line bet and the Odds bet. In this example, you could lose $20 or win $22. If the Point has been Four or Ten you could have lost $20 or won $30. Had the Point been Five or Nine, you could have lost $20 or won $25.

The reason the payoffs are different for the various Point numbers is that some are more difficult to throw than others (see Figures 2 and 3).

Are you a step ahead of me at this time? Yes, Come bets-Odds bets are identical to Pass Line odds bets. They are made in the same manner, they win or lose in the same manner, they have the same payoffs. Here are the only differences:

1) As stated earlier, your Come bet can be made only *after* a Come-out roll.

2) Instead of playing your Odds bet on the table, you hand your chips to the dealer and say, "Odds on my Come Point." If you come Point (for example) was Eight, you could also say, "Come Odds on the Eight." The dealer will then place your Odds bet on top of and slightly out of line with your Come bet.

DON'T PASS-ODDS BETS

First you must make a wager on Don't Pass. Then, if a Point is rolled, you can back up your Don't Pass bet by laying the odds on the Point. Since you are laying, rather than taking, the odds, the payoffs are reversed.

1) If the Point is Four or Ten, the payoff is one to two. A $6 wage would pay $3.

2) If the Point is Five or Nine, the payoff is two to three. A $6 wager would pay $4.

3) If the Point is Six or Eight, the payoff is five to six. A $6 wager would pay $5.

Please note that this bet should be made in multiples of $6 to ensure proper payoffs.

To make this bet, place your chips for the Odds bet immediately adjacent to your Don't Pass bet, or on top of your Don't Pass bet at a slight offset. If you do it wrong, the dealer will show you how.

If the Point is rolled before a Seven, you lose both

your Don't Pass and Odds bets. If a Seven is rolled before the Point, you win both your Don't Pass and Odds bets.

DON'T COME-ODDS BETS

Right again. Don't Come-Odds bets are identical to Don't Pass-Odds bets. They are made in the same manner, they win or lose in the same manner, they have the same payoffs. Here are the only differences:

1) As stated earlier, your Don't Come bet can be made only *after* a Come-out roll.
2) Instead of placing your Odds bet on the table, you hand your chips to the dealer and say, "Odds on the Don't Come," or words to that effect. The dealer will then place your Odds bet in the Don't Come section of the Box just above your Don't Come Point.

Again, the overall casino advantage on Pass Line, Don't Pass, Come, or Don't Come is about 1.4%. If you take or lay the corresponding Odds bets, the casino advantage is reduced to about .8%.

Now let's investigate your other alternatives.

PLACE BETS

These bets can only be made on the numbers Four, Five, Six, Eight, Nine or Ten. Do not make this bet yourself! Hand your chips to the dealer and tell him what numbers you want to place. You may place any or all of the numbers, you may make or remove this bet at any time. When you want to remove your bet, tell the dealer "Off my Place bets," or "My Place bets are off."

See if you can follow the intent of this rule: Unless the player makes a request for the Place bets to be off, they are always on for all rolls except the Come-out roll, when they are always off unless requested to be on. Sound confusing? To clarify matters, it is to your advantage for Place bets to be on at all times. Whether you win or lose a Place bet is determined in the following manner:

1) If a Seven is rolled before your Place number, you lose.
2) If your Place number is rolled before a Seven, you win.

Here are the payoffs:

Four and Ten pay nine to five

Five and Nine pay seven to five

Six and Eight pay seven to six

Please note that these payoffs are less than the payoffs for Free Odds bets associated with pass, Don't Pass, Come, and Don't Come. Not a lot less, but enough to increase the casino's advantage. On Four and Ten the casino's advantage is about 6.7%. For Five and Nine it is 4%. For six and Eight it is only about 1.5%, which makes Six and Eight the best numbers to place.

BUY BETS

Buy bets are very similar to Place bets. As with Place bets, you are essentially wagering that the shooter will roll your number before a Seven. Buy bets can be made or removed at any time; they are made on the same numbers as Place bets, and you make the bet by handing your chips to the dealer. But now you say, "Buy the Eight," or "Buy the Four." The similarities end with the above. Here are differences:

1) A small marker, which looks as if it came from a tiddlywinks game, is set on top of your chips

to distinguish your Buy bet from a place bet. The marker has "Buy" stamped on it.

2) The payoffs are different:

Four and Ten pay two to one

Five and Nine pay three to two

Six and Eight pay six to five

3) On Buy bets the casino charges a five percent service charge in multiples of $1. If you want to bet $10, it will cost you $11. A bet of $20 would cost $21. A $40 bet would cost $42 ($40 x 5% = $2). The charge is always in multiples of $1 because the casino does not give change of fifty cents or twenty-five cents.

The casino advantage on buy bets is approximately 5%, so this is not a great bet for the player.

LAY BETS

This wager is nearly the exact opposite of a Buy bet. You are betting that the shooter will roll a Seven before your Lay number. You can make a Lay bet on the Four, Five, Six, Eight, Nine or Ten. Give the dealer your chips and say, "Lay the odds on Six" or "Lay the Eight." The dealer will place your chips in the Don't Come section of the number you request, then put a small Buy marker on top of them. Lay bets are always on, even on the Come-out roll. If a Seven is rolled before your number, the payoffs are:

Four and Ten pay one to two

Five and Nine pay two to three

Six and Eight pay five to six

As with Buy bets, there is a five percent service charge involved, but the five percent is based on your potential winnings instead of on your bet.

Example: You want to make a $40 Lay bet on the Four. If you were to win, the payoff would be $20. Five percent of $20 is $1, which is added to the cost of your bet. So, in order to be paid correctly on a bet of $40, you need to bet $41. Sound dumb? The casino advantage on Lay bets is 2.5% on the Four and Ten, 3.2% on the Five and Nine, 4% on the Six or Eight. If you want to try a Lay bet, make it on the Four or Ten.

BIG SIX OR BIG EIGHT

This is another wager which can be made or removed at any time. It is also another bad bet. You can make this bet by yourself by placing chips in the Big Six or Big Eight portion of the table layout. Your bet is won or lost in the following manner:

1) If Six or Eight (depending on which you bet) is rolled before Seven, you win even money.
2) If Seven is thrown before Six or Eight, you lose.

Here's why this is a bad bet. Six and Eight can each be rolled in five combinations. Seven can be rolled in six combinations. The true payoff for this wager, therefore, should be six to five instead of even money. By paying even money the casino reaps an advantage of 9.09%!

Note: In Atlantic City this bet is paid off at seven to six, which lowers the casino advantage to 1.5%. This is much better for the player, but all bets should be made in multiples of $6.

HARD TEN OR HARD FOUR

I've lumped these two together because the payoffs and

probabilities are the same for both numbers. They are two separate bets which can be made by handing chips to the *stickman*, who controls all bets in the center of the table. This bet can be made or removed at any time.

Hard Four can only be rolled one way (two, two). Hard Ten can only be rolled one way (five, five). You are betting that Hard Four or Hard Ten (whichever you choose) will be rolled before Seven, *and* before any other combination of Four or Ten.

The payoff is seven to one, which sounds juicy. But let's say you bet the hard Four. Only one combination can win for you: (two, two). *Eight* combinations will lose the bet — six combinations of Seven, plus (one, three) and (three, one). The true payoff should be eight to one, but since the casino only pays seven to one its advantage is 11.1%!

HARD SIX OR HARD EIGHT

This bet is also made through the stickman; it may be placed or removed before any roll. The payoffs and probabilities are the same for both. If you make a bet on Hard Six you are wagering that (three, three) will be rolled before any Seven, *and also* before any other combination of Six. The payoff is nine to one.

But Hard Six can only be rolled in one way, while there are six combinations of Seven and four others of Six: (one, five), (two, four), (four, two), or (five, one). One way can win, ten will lose. The true payoff should be ten to one, but since the casino only pay nine to one their advantage on this one is 9.09%.

ONE ROLL BETS

All of the following wagers are decided by one roll of the dice. After making these wagers, the very next roll will cause you to win or lose. With the lone exception of the Field bet, which you can easily place for yourself, all of these bets are made through the stickman. If you want action on each roll of the dice, here's your chance.

Field Bets

This bet is very popular because seven different outcomes (Two, Three, Four, Nine, Ten, Eleven, or Twelve) can win, while only four (Five, Six, Seven, or Eight) can lose. However, the winning numbers can be rolled in a total of only sixteen ways. The losing numbers can be rolled in twenty ways. You have a 44.4% chance of winning and a 55.6% chance of losing. That means that the casino has an 11.2% advantage.

The odds improve when the casino pays two to one or three to one when a Two or a Twelve is rolled, but the odds are still stacked against you. You might get lucky for a few rolls, but over the long haul the casino edge will grind you down.

Any Seven

Here you are betting that the next roll will be a Seven. Since there are six ways to roll a Seven, there are six combinations which will win for you. The other thirty possible outcomes will lose for you. The true payoff on this bet should be five to one (thirty to six), but since the casino only pays four to one its advantage is 16.7%.

Any Craps

Now you're betting that the next roll will be with Two, Three, or Twelve. Two can be rolled in one way, Three can be rolled in two ways, Twelve can be rolled in one way. Four outcomes can win for you; the other thirty-two will cause a loss. The true payoff should be eight to one, but since the casino only pays seven to one its advantage on this bet is 11.1%.

Two

Another poor wager. You are betting that the next roll will be a Two. The payoff is thirty to one, which sounds very enticing.

But Two can only be rolled in one way. Only one outcome can win for you, the other thirty-five cause a loss. The true payoff should be thirty-five to one, but since the casino only pays thirty to one its advantage is a very nice (for the casino) 13.9%.

Twelve

Same as Two, above.

Three

Now you're betting that the next roll will be a Three. The payoff is fifteen to one. But Three can only be rolled in two ways. Two combinations can win for your, thirty-four can lose. The true payoff should be seventeen to one, but since the casino only pay fifteen to one its advantage is 11.8%.

Eleven

Same as Three, above.

Craps-Eleven (Also Called a Horn Bet)

This one is even worse than all the others. Here you're wagering that a Two, a Three, an Eleven or a Twelve will show on the next roll. The payoffs are as follows:

Two pays thirty to one

Three pays fifteen to one

Eleven pays fifteen to one

Twelve pays thirty to one

Since you're covering four numbers, you must bet four chips. From our earlier discussion, you already know that the payoffs for all these numbers are incorrect, giving the casino ad advantage of from 11.8% to 13.9%. In addition, even if you win on one of the numbers, you still lose your other three chips, which makes the casino advantage even higher. If you like these kinds of odds, perhaps you should try Russian Roulette.

DOUBLE AND TRIPLE ODDS

I am referring to the Odds bets which can be made in conjunction with Pass Line, Come, Don't Pass, and Don't Come wagers. Many casinos allow these Odds bets to be made in double or triple the amount of your initial wager.

Example: You are playing at a table which offers Double Odds. Your Pass Line bet is $10. A Point is established. You may now wager up to $20 on the associated Odds bet. If you were playing at a Triple Odds table, your Pass Line Odds bet could be as high as $20.

Both Double and Triple Odds reduce the casino's advantage, but don't get carried away. One bad spell of luck at a Double or Triple Odds table will quickly demolish your gambling stake.

WAGERING LIMITS

Minimum wagers at most Crap tables will be either $2 or $5 with the maximum running up to $1000 or $2000. I suggest that you start at a $2 table until you gain confidence. Then, if you want more action, most casinos will allow you to make an Odds bet which is greater than your original Pass Line, Come, Don't Pass or Don't Come bet.

Example: If your original wager is three units ($3, $6, $9, $12, $15, and so forth), your associated Odds bet can be four units if the Point is Five or Nine, five units if the Point is Six or Eight.

Example: You bet $15 on the Pass Line. The Come-out roll is a Six, which becomes the Point. Since you bet three units (three units of $5 = $15) on Pass Line, you may now bet five units ($25) on your associated Odds bet.

All this can be very confusing, so make certain you know the exact bets allowed by the casino. For most of us, it is difficult to remember betting units, payoffs, and how to make the proper bets to ensure accurate payoffs without becoming bewildered. After reading this chapter you should have enough knowledge to play Craps with confidence. But, as I also mentioned when discussing Blackjack, none of your knowledge of Craps means anything unless you manage your money properly. You can make all the right bets and still lose money — lots of money. To help prevent severe losses, I offer the following suggestions:

1) Start with at least 50 units. 75 units would be more practical.

2) Change tables if you lose 5-10 units. A fresh table can give you fresh enthusiasm. If your casino only has one or two Crap tables open, then change casinos.

3) If you win as many as 10 units at any table, *do not* lose it back! As soon as you start winning, put your original chips in your pocket and play

with your winnings, then leave the table before the casino can recapture its losses.

4) If you win as many as 25 units, increase your unit. If you win 40 units, increase your unit again.

5) Make only the wagers on which the casino has the lowest advantage. These include: Pass Line and Odds, Don't Pass and Odds, Come bets and Odds, Don't Come and Odds, Place the Six or Eight.

6) Regardless of whether you bet Pass Line, Come, Don't Pass or Don't Come, always take or lay the associated Odds bets, if you can afford it. While this can cause you to lose twice as fast, you can also win more and reduce the casino's edge from 1.4% to .8%.

7) Do not switch your bets back and forth in an attempt to catch a good or bad run of the dice. If you are betting the pass Line, stay with it. If you are betting Don't Come, stay with it. If you switch back and forth you may get caught between flip-flopping dice and lose every bet. Most good gamblers follow this rule and find it lessens frustration.

8) Do not double your bet after a loss. If you lose six or seven consecutive bets, which is entirely possible, you will blow your whole gambling stake.

9) Develop a game plan before you start betting. Know *how* you want to bet, *what* you want to bet, and the payoffs. Stick to those basic wagers until your knowledge is complete. Then,

and only then, should you experiment with any exotic bets. Probably the greatest difficulty in playing Craps is that with so much action taking place, with so many people screaming, with so many chips flying around, it is very easy to get confused. Do not rush yourself! You do not have to place a bet on every roll of the dice. If you make a mistake on a bet, such as placing your chips in the wrong area, the casino will not show you any sympathy.

10) Whenever you are in doubt, seek the assistance of the dealers. It is in their job to assist you. There is no such thing as a stupid question. In fact, it is in your best interest to develop a rapport with the dealers. Treat them with respect and you'll receive all the help you need.

That's all for this chapter, but don't forget to read and study the practical advice at the end of this book, which includes a suggestion on betting strategy.

3

BACCARAT

IF YOU ARE A PERSON who desires the simplest of card games, Baccarat is for you. There are only three player options:

1) You can bet on the banker's hand.

2) You can bet on the player's hand.

3) You can bet on Tie.

And since a bet on Tie is a foolish wager, you can narrow down the options to just two: bet on players or bankers. Yes, the game really is that simple.

Yet, even though Baccarat is easy to play, most people assume you need to be a millionaire and have superior intelligence in order to sit at a Baccarat table. Not so, not so. All you need is money.

Most every casino has at least one Baccarat table, with the betting limits ranging from $20 to $2000 or

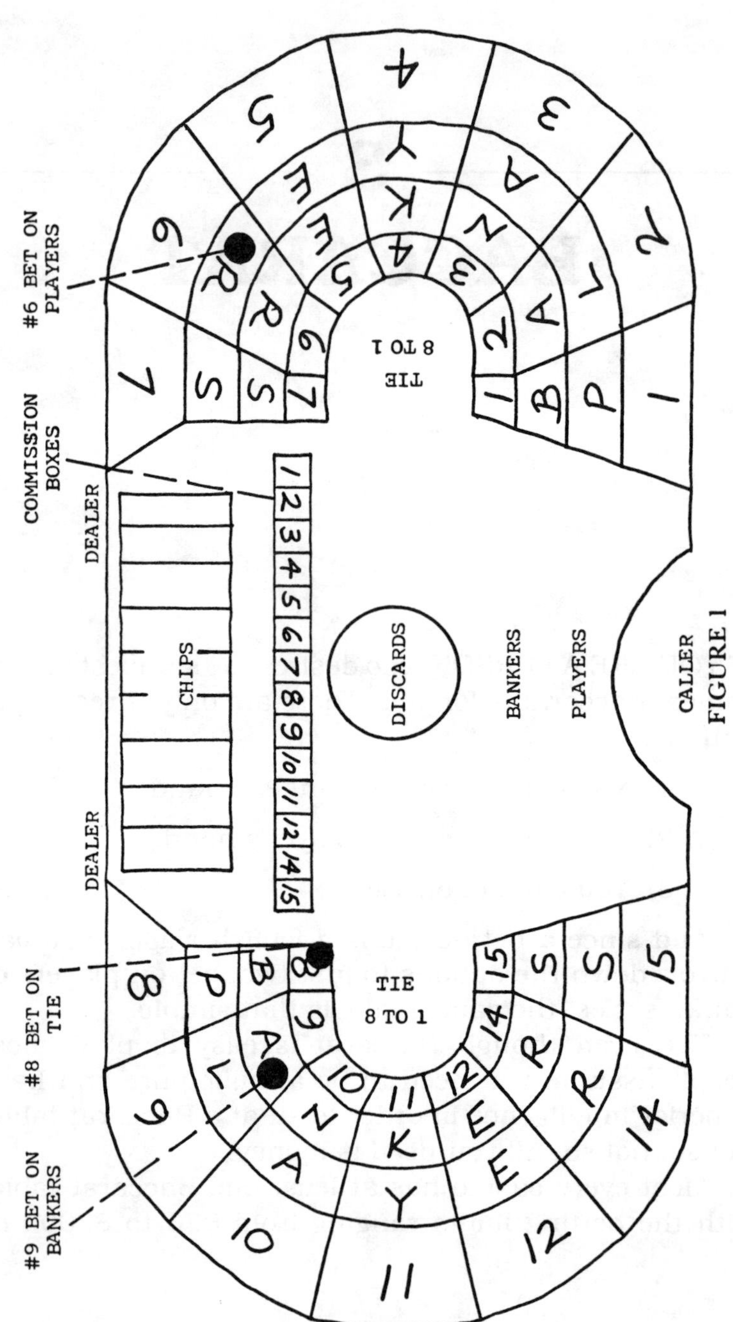
#6 BET ON PLAYERS
COMMISSION BOXES
DEALER
DEALER
#8 BET ON TIE
#9 BET ON BANKERS
CHIPS
DISCARDS
BANKERS
PLAYERS
CALLER
TIE 8 TO 1
TIE 8 TO 1
PLAYERS
BANKERS

FIGURE 1

more. Perhaps a minimum wager if $20 scares a lot of people away from the game. I'm sure it does. But if you can afford to wager $20 on each round of play, Baccarat offers very little disadvantage to the player, with the casino's advantage ranging from only 1.2% to about 1.4%. So let's take a good look at this game.

Trudging through the casino one evening you note that one gaming area is situated off to the side of the room, either partitioned or roped off from the rest of the gambling areas, making the activities in that room seem very private. Upon closer inspection you see men in tuxedos, beautiful women in evening dresses, posh decorations. It looks glamorous, exotic, mysterious. There's even a man in a chair perched high over the action. Other spectators grouped near you are trying to watch the play, a look of awe in their eyes. But, being slightly different from the majority, you are not satisfied with watching. Even though you're dressed in denims and a cowboy shirt, you hold your head erect, jut out your chin and march into that room as if you owned the casino. A few of the gamblers sitting at the table glance at you with expressionless faces as you take the first open seat you see.

As with all other casino games, your first step is to purchase chips. Then before making any wagers, you study the table layout (see Figure 1).

Assume you're at seat number 1. Note that there are only three compartments where you can place a wager, all of which are within easy reach directly in front of your position. Two of the casino employees (dealers), both sitting on the same side of the table, are shuffling eight decks of cards. For the moment, there is nothing for you to do. You can lean back in your comfortable chair and relax.

After a short time, the dealers are finished shuffling

the cards and a ritual begins. One of the dealers hands you a plain plastic card and moves all eight decks in your direction. Being astute, you quickly determine that he wants you to cut the cards. You insert the plastic card into the stack of cards; the dealer cuts the decks at that point and then places all eight decks into a plastic shoe similar to those at the Blackjack tables. So far, so good. The other players assume that you know what you're doing.

Next, the dealer removes the first card from the shoe and shows it to the players. It is a Six. You say, "Big deal," with sarcasm filling your voice. Ah, you just labeled yourself as a novice. The dealer frowns at your ignorance of Baccarat custom and then removes six more cards from the shoe, placing them in a discard slot in the middle of the table. If the first card had been a Four, four cards would have been discarded. Get the picture? The numbers of cards which are "burned" is determined by the first card out of the shoe. This helps prevent cheating.

You then expect the dealer to slide the cards out to the players, but something strange happens. The dealer shoves the entire plastic shoe in front of your position. You think: "My God, what now?"

Well, you've just become the banker. And no, that does not mean you have to pay off all the winning bets when the game starts. It simply means you're going to be the dealer for a while. Like a lot of other people, you have confused Baccarat with Chemin-de-Fer because of the James Bond movie *Goldfinger*. In Baccarat the *casino* collects and pays off — not the banker. You issue a sigh of relief.

But since you're the banker, you *must* make a bet. You can bet on bankers or players, but most players bet on bankers when they have the shoe. The person with the shoe is the banker, so most bankers bet on bankers. Make sense? You don't have to be the banker if you don't want to be. If you don't want to deal the cards, simply say "No thanks," or words to that effect. The shoe will then be offered to the person on your right.

Okay, you decide you want to deal, so you place the minimum wager of $20 on bankers. For a moment, you wonder how you'll be able to deal cards to the players at the other end of the table, but another casino employee standing opposite the dealers solves the problem for you. He is the "caller," the person who directs the play of the game. He instructs you to deal him a card, then one to yourself, then another to him, then another to yourself, all face down. The first and third cards form the player's hand, the second and fourth form the banker's hand. Right. There are only two hands: the banker's and the player's.

Now more ritual. The caller passes his two cards, the player's hand, to a lady sitting at the far end of the table who has $2000 wagered on the player's hand. The reason he gave them to her is because she had the largest bet on players. The lady turns the cards over, face up, then passes them back to the caller, who places them face up on the table in front of him. You wonder why the caller couldn't just turn the cards over by himself, but you keep quiet.

The caller then turns to you and directs you to turn over the banker's hand. You do so, seeing a Six and a Nine. Because of your Blackjack experience, you assume that the hand is worth a total of 15. The woman next to you murmurs "Five." Your first impulse is to tell your fellow gambler that she is wrong, that the banker's total is 15, not 5. However, being a novice, you keep your mouth shut. And it's good that you didn't say anything. For, you see, it is impossible for any hand to total more than 9. Aces are counted as one. Tens, Jacks, Queens and Kings are counted as zero. All other cards are face value; for example, a Six is worth six, a Five is worth five. If the total of the cards is a two-digit number, like 15, the first digit is dropped. So 15 becomes 5. If the total were 25, the hand would still be 5.

At the caller's request, you pass the banker's hand to him. He places the banker's hand on the table in front of him, just slightly above the player's hand.

Did you win or lose? You don't know yet. The banker's hand is 5, and assume that the player's hand is 4. But, the way this game is played, the player's hand may need another card, the banker's hand may need another card, both may need another, or neither may need another. In any case, neither hand can have more than three cards. The beauty of Baccarat is that the decision as to whether either hand receives another card is not yours to make. The caller is in charge of the game. He will tell you if either hand needs another card, basing his decisions on the very strict rules which govern this game. You may request a copy of the printed rules and the casino will be happy to oblige you.

In this case the caller says to you, "A card for players." You deal the card face down to the caller, who places it face up adjacent to the player's hand. The player's hand is always acted upon before the banker's hand. The card is a Seven, increasing the player's hand to 11, which is really one 1. But you're not done yet.

The caller tells you, "A card for bankers." You dutifully slip another card out of the shoe, face down, and pass it to the caller. He turns it over adjacent to the banker's other two cards. It is a Three, giving the banker's hand a total of 18, which is really just 8. Remember? You always drop the first digit of a two-digit total.

The caller then announces, "Bankers win, eight over one." The two dealers collect the losing bets on players and pay off the winning bets on bankers. But as the dealer on your side of the table pays off your bet on bankers, you notice that he is also placing a little chip in a row of boxes in front of him. More specifically, he places one of those chips in the box marked 1, which is your position. Don't be alarmed. When you bet on bankers and win, you must pay the casino a five percent commission. The dealer is simply keeping track of how much commission you owe. He will collect the commission later, before you leave the table or after the last hand is played from the shoe.

I know a five percent commission on winnings sounds terrible, but what you don't know yet is that the rules governing the game favor the banker's hand. Consequently, the banker's hand wins more often than the player's hand. Because of this, the casino must charge a commission to make any money. Had you bet on players and won, you wouldn't have paid any commission. If you don't want to pay commissions, just bet on players all the time. But, as I stated, bankers win more often than players.

Now, does that sound like a difficult game? Of course not. The most difficult part was being the banker (dealer), and all you had to do was follow the caller's instructions. Had you not been the banker, you would have simply placed a bet, relaxed, and awaited the outcome.

Let's take this example a step further. You deal another hand in the same manner as the first. But this time players win. All that happens is that you pass the shoe to the person on your right. The shoe changes whenever the banker's hand loses, and travels around the table counter-clockwise. It keeps moving until the plain plastic card shows up — the same plastic card that you inserted into the decks at the beginning. That hand is played out to completion; then the decks are either reshuffled or eight new decks are introduced.

Assume that you bet on bankers sixteen times, and won fourteen times. You bet $20 on each hand. Now it's time to pay your commission. $20 x 14 winning hands = $280. 5% of $280 = $14. Is that so terrible? Of course not, especially since the rules favor bankers.

The chart depicted below shows the rules administered by the caller, but you needn't memorize them. You have no control, anyway. You simply bet on bankers or players and either win or lose. While it's possible for the caller to make a mistake, that possibility is very remote.

The idea of the game is to get a total of 9, or as close to 9 as possible. Whichever hand is closer to 9 is the winner. If either hand is dealt 8 or 99 on the first two cards, that hand has a Natural. If one hand has a Natural and the other doesn't, the Natural wins automatically. If one has 8, the other 9, the 9 wins the hand. Once a natural is revealed, that round is over.

Now let's look at a few sample hands.

Example #1. Players is dealt a Queen and a Ten. Bankers is dealt a Two and a Three. What happens now? Well, refer to the rules. The player's total is 0, so players must draw another card. Say that players receives a Six, for a total of 6. And since players drew a Six, for a total of 6. And since players drew a Six, bankers must also take an additional card. Say that bankers draws a Seven, for a total of 12, which is really just 2, and loses the round. The caller says, "Players wins, six over two."

Example #2. Players receives a Six and a Five. Bankers receives a Ten and a Seven. What happens next? Again, refer to the rules. If the player's total is 1, players must draw a card. But what does bankers do with a total

PLAYER'S RULES

IF PLAYER'S TWO-CARD TOTAL IS	PLAYER MUST
0, 1, 2, 3, 4, 5	DRAW
6, 7	STAND
8, 9	NATURAL**

**A Natural is an automatic winner unless the banker's two-card total is also 8 or 9, in which case a tie could be the result.

FIGURE 2

of 7? Well, if bankers has a total of 7, it does not make any difference what card players draws. Bankers *must* stand on 7. Even if players draws an Eight, for a total of 9, bankers still can't draw another card. Yes, even though it means bankers will lose the round.

Example #3. Player's total is 4. Banker's total is 4. Players must draw a card, does, and receives a Three for a total of 7. And since players drew a Three, bankers must draw a card also.

Example #4. Again, players and bankers each have a total of 4. But this time the player's hand draws a Queen, and therefore does not improve its total. Can

FIGURE 3

BANKER'S RULES

BANKER'S TWO-CARD TOTAL	DRAWS CARD IF PLAYER DRAWS A	DOES NOT DRAW IF PLAYER DRAWS A
0, 1, 2	MUST DRAW	MUST DRAW
3	0,1,2,3,4,5,6,7,9	8
4	2,3,4,5,6,7	0,1,8,9
5	4,5,6,7	0,1,2,3,8,9
6	6,7	0,1,2,3,4,5,8,9
7	MUST STAND	MUST STAND
8,9	NATURAL**	NATURAL**

**A Natural is an automatic winner unless the player's hand is also a Natural.

bankers now take another card? No. The round would end in a tie.

Example #5. Player's hand receives a King and a Jack. Banker's hand catches an Ace and a Ten. Player's hand totals 20, which is really just 0. Banker's hand totals 11, which is really just 1. Players must draw an additional card, does, and receives another Jack. Player's hand is still worth only 0. You've bet on bankers, so you think you've won the hand 1 over 0. But, alas, any time the banker's hand has a total of 0, 1, or 2, bankers must draw a card. In this example, bankers could possibly turn a winning hand into a losing hand by taking an additional card, but that's the rules, folks.

Now the next time you have an extra $100 in your pocket you can bounce into the Baccarat area and play at least five bets. You can sit there and sip your drink, cast looks of disdain at the spectators on the other side of the ropes, and feel like a high roller. What the hell? Go ahead and do it at least once in your life.

Remember how simple it is. You bet on bankers or players. It's really that easy. Who knows? You might get lucky. Baccarat attracts many wealthy gamblers, so you can bet the minimum and watch the high rollers win or lose hundreds of thousands of dollars. Next time, instead of marveling at what is happening in that small private room, join the action.

The best thing about this game is that it is entirely possible to win more than you lose, even if you play the five percent commission. The casino's advantage on players is about 1.4%. On bankers (including the commission), the casino's advantage is only 1.2%, which makes a bet on bankers one of the best wagers in the casino.

Oh, yes. I forgot to tell you. That person hovering over the game from his tall, tall chair is called the ladderman.

It is his job to oversee the game and watch for cheating and collusion between dealers and players. Unless you're trying to cheat, ignore him.

MINI-BACCARAT

As the term implies, Mini-Baccarat is a smaller version of the same game. It is played at a smaller table (normally found near the Blackjack tables), allows a smaller minimum wager ($2-$5), and one dealer does everything; the dealing, the exchanging of chips on wins or losses, the calling of the hands.

There aren't many of these tables available, but they are a good place to start if you can find one. Play Mini-Baccarat until you gain confidence, then move on to the big table.

However, exercise some care. In Baccarat, as played on the big tables, you don't lose ties. If you bet on either bankers or players and the result is a tie, you don't win or lose unless you have bet on Tie. But in quite a few of the Mini-Baccarat games the casino wins all ties. This rule is bad for gamblers, so watch out for it.

Also, the minimum commission charged on a winning wager on bankers is usually twenty-five cents. So even if you wagered only two dollars, which should mean a commission of ten cents, you still must pay twenty-five cents. Not much difference, but those nickels and dimes add up in a hurry.

MONEY MANAGEMENT

Due to the larger minimum wager required for this game, I suggest that there are only two times when you should play Baccarat:

1) If you have at least $100 fun money to blow.

2) If you purchase the books which I recommend at the end of this book, study the Baccarat systems offered in those books, and can play with a bankroll of at least $5000.

Note: In Atlantic City you may have difficulty finding a $20 game. In an effort to make Baccarat even more exclusive, the casinos in Atlantic City often require a minimum wager of $40, $60 or more, with a frequent minimum of $100.

4

ROULETTE

WHO WOULD HAVE THOUGHT that a large wheel and small ball could cause the loss of millions of dollars? Defined in most dictionaries as a gambling game in which players bet on which compartment of a revolving wheel a small ball will come to rest in, the game is easy to learn, easy to play.

A dealer (croupier) oversees the betting, makes the pay-offs, rotates the wheel and spins the ivory ball. If the ball drops into the compartment housing one of the numbers that you've bet, you win. There is no mystique to this game. The wheel rotates, the ball spins, you win or lose.

I have not supplied a diagram of a Roulette wheel since a few moments' observation of one can tell you all you need to know. The only difference between Roulette wheels is that some have only 0 and others have 0 *and* 00. However, unless you leave the United States, all wheels will have both 0 and 00. All wheels in the world also have the numbers 1-36, eighteen of which are red, eighteen of which are black; 0 and 00 normally have a green background. The red numbers are 1, 3, 5, 7, 9, 12, 14, 16, 18, 19, 21, 23, 25, 27, 30, 32, 34 and 36. The black numbers are 2, 4, 6, 8, 10, 11, 13, 15, 17, 20, 22, 24, 26, 28, 29, 31, 33 and 35. Consequently, there are 38 compartments on each American wheel. According to the law of averages, each number should come up once every 38 spins. Unfortunately, the wheel and ball do not understand the law of averages.

I once spent an entire evening noting the results of each spin at a Roulette table. I did not make any wagers; I simply jotted down the outcomes of each spin. Mentally, I was betting on number 32, but I did not actually place a bet. Good thing, too. For had I actually been

FIGURE 1
ROULETTE BETTING LAYOUT

00	3	6	9	12	15	18	21	24	27	30	33	36	2 to 1
	2	5	8	11	14	17	20	23	26	29	32	35	2 to 1
0	1	4	7	10	13	16	19	22	25	28	31	34	2 to 1
	1st 12				2nd 12				3rd 12				
	1 to 18		EVEN		RED		BLACK		ODD		19 to 36		

wagering on number 32, I would have lost money. Number 32 was the result on the fifth spin after I arrived at the table, but it did not repeat again until the 147th spin of the wheel. Had I been wagering real money, I would have bet 147 units and won back only 70. Yet during that same time period, the number 00 came up on *twelve* spins. Had I wagered on 00 I would have bet 147 units and won 420 units. The point is this: If the law of averages had held completely true, both 32 and 00 would have been the result about four times each. But, as I've already mentioned in other sections, the law of averages is not based on 38 spins. It is based on millions of spins. So it is possible to sit at a Roulette table all night without seeing your favorite number appear. Conversely, it is also possible to see your favorite number appear many, many times. And that's why we play this silly game, isn't it?

Your first step is to purchase chips. If you already have chips from playing one of the other casino games, you can use them to make your roulette wagers, but it is more advisable to purchase Roulette chips; in fact, you may be asked to do so. If three people each bet a red casino $5 chip and one of them wins, who does the dealer pay? How does the dealer know which chip belongs to which player? Avoid this potential problem by purchasing Roulette chips. These chips are designed especially for Roulette; each player who buys them receives a different color, and you can assign to them whatever money value you want.

Example: You are going to play at a table which requires a $2 minimum bet. You want to buy $20 in chips. Depending on the casino's rules, you might obtain (at your request) twenty $1 chips, forty chips worth fifty cents each, or eighty chips worth twenty-five cents each. The dealer may give you orange chips, purple

FIGURE 2

TYPE OF WAGER	ACTUAL PAYOFF	TRUE ODDS	CASINO ADVANTAGE
ONE NUMBER	35:1	37:1	5.26%
TWO NUMBERS	17:1	18:1	5.26%
THREE NUMBERS	11:1	11.7:1	5.26%
FOUR NUMBERS	8:1	8.5:1	5.26%
FIVE NUMBERS	6:1	6.6:1	7.89%
SIX NUMBERS	5:1	5.3:1	5.26%
DOZENS	2:1	2.2:1	5.26%
COLUMNS	2:1	2.2:1	5.26%
RED OR BLACK	1:1	1.1:1	5.26%
ODD OR EVEN	1:1	1.1:1	5.26%
1-18 OR 19-36	1:1	1.1:1	5.26%

chips or yellow chips, but, whichever you receive, you will be the *only* person at the Roulette table with that color. And the dealer will mark your chips, so there will be no misunderstanding as to whether you are playing with chips worth fifty cents, twenty-five cents, or some other value.

Roulette chips can be used only at a Roulette table. You purchase them from the dealer, you sell them back to the dealer before you leave the table. *Do not* leave the table with the chips! If you try to take them from one table to another, they will not be honored by the new dealer, since the new dealer does not know what value your chips have been assigned.

Once you have chips, your betting options are numerous, each wager winning or losing on the very next spin of the wheel. Figure 2 is a list of the options, along with the casino's advantage for each bet.

Actual payoffs are what you actually receive if you win one of the above wagers. True odds indicate what the payoffs *should be*. The difference between the two is the casino's advantage. As you can see, the Five Number bet is the worst that you can place.

INSIDE BETS

These bets can only be made in the portion of the betting layout seen in Figure 3.

FIGURE 3

00	3	6	9	12	15	18	21	24	27	30	33	36
	2	5	8	11	14	17	20	23	26	29	32	35
0	1	4	7	10	13	16	19	22	25	28	31	34

The reason that these bets are classified as Inside bets is because the maximum amount that you wager differs from what are known as Outside bets (described later). Always ask the dealer about the maximum wager when you buy your Roulette chips. Though the table may advertise a $500 maximum, this does not necessarily mean you can make a $500 bet. The amount you can wager on an Inside bet varies from casino to casino. Usually, the maximum wager on a One Number bet is $25. However, a $25 bet on a single number would pay $875. Obviously, if the casino allowed $500 wagers on single numbers, where the payoff would be $17,500, a person on a lucky streak could quickly force a closing of the table.

Also: If you are playing at a $2 table, you must make bets *totaling* $2. You do not need to bet the entire $2 on just one bet. If you were playing with chips worth fifty cents, you could make four different bets. In other words, your $2 could be spread all over the betting layout.

All of the following are Inside Bets:

One Number Bets

FIGURE 4

00	3	6	9	12	15	18	21	24	27	30	33	36
	2	5	8	11	14	17	20	23	26	29	32	35
0	1	4	7	10	13	16	19	22	25	28	31	34

Figure 4 shows five different One Number bets (00, 8, 13, 21, and 29). Simply make sure your chips are clearly placed within the boundaries of the number or numbers you select. Since there are 38 numbers on the betting layout, there are 38 different ways to make this bet. You can wager on as many numbers as you like.

Note: As with all other Roulette bets, it is permissible to place your chips on top of the chips of other players. Do not be alarmed if someone stacks five blue chips atop your purple ones. If you are wagering more than one chip on a bet, stack your chips on top of each other.

Two Number Bets

FIGURE 5

00	3	6	9	12	15	18	21	24	27	30	33	36
	2	5	8	11	14	17	20	23	26	29	32	35
0	1	4	7	10	13	16	19	22	25	28	31	34

The two numbers you select must be adjacent. There are 62 different ways to place this bet. Figure 5 shows three ways (0, 00 or 8, 9 or 14, 17). You could *not* cover numbers such as 2, 16 or 23, 26 since they are not adjacent.

Three Number Bets

FIGURE 6

00	3	6	9	12	15	18	21	24	27	30	33	36
	2	5	8	11	14	17	20	23	26	29	32	35
0	1	4	7	10	13	16	19	22	25	28	31	34

All of the bets in Figure 6 cover three numbers each (1, 0, 2 or 0, 2, 00 or 2, 00, 3 or 7, 8, 9 or 31, 32, 33). In all, this bet can be made in fifteen different ways.

Four Number Bets

FIGURE 7

00	3	6	9	12	15	18	21	24	27	30	33	36
	2	5	8	11	14	17	20	23	26	29	32	35
0	1	4	7	10	13	16	19	22	25	28	31	34

The three wagers shown in Figure 7 (2, 3, 5, 6 or 14, 15, 17, 18 or 4, 5, 7, 8) are all Four number bets. In this example, if 5 were the result on the next spin you would be paid twice at the eight to one rate because 5 is covered in two different bets. There are 22 ways to make this wager.

Five number Bet

There is only *one* Five Number Bet. It is indicated in Figure 8 and can be made by placing your wager in *either* of the positions depicted. As you saw in Figure 2, this is

FIGURE 8

00	3	6	9	12	15	18	21	24	27	30	33	36
	2	5	8	11	14	17	20	23	26	29	32	35
0	1	4	7	10	13	16	19	22	25	28	31	34

the worst possible wager for the player. The bet covers 0, 1, 2, 3, and 00.

Six Number Bets

FIGURE 9

00	3	6	9	12	15	18	21	24	27	30	33	36
	2	5	8	11	14	17	20	23	26	29	32	35
0	1	4	7	10	13	16	19	22	25	28	31	34

There are eleven of these bets, three of which are shown in Figure 9. The first chip covers 1, 2, 3, 4, 5, and 6. The second chip covers 10, 11, 12, 13, 14, 15. The Third covers 19, 20, 21, 22, 23, 24.

OUTSIDE BETS

These bets can only be made in the portion of the betting

FIGURE 10

						2-1
						2-1
						2-1
1st 12		2nd 12		3rd 12		
1 to 18	EVEN	RED	BLACK	ODD	19 to 36	

layout shown in Figure 10. Some of these wagers are paid off at two to one, the rest at even money, but you can only wager the table maximum on those which pay even money.

Dozens

FIGURE 11

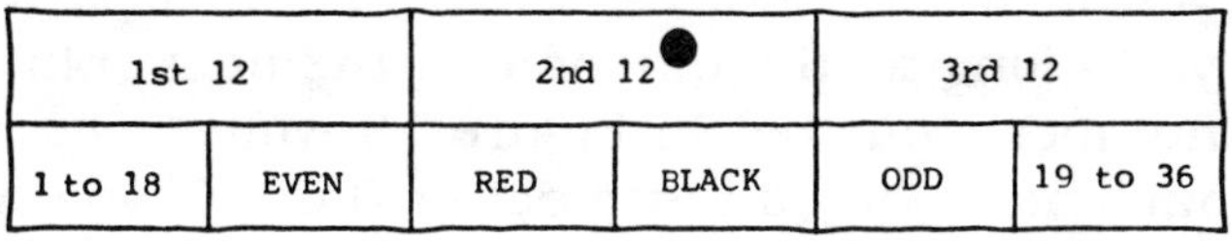

1st 12		2nd 12 ●		3rd 12	
1 to 18	EVEN	RED	BLACK	ODD	19 to 36

There are only three ways to make this bet. Figure 11 shows a bet covering the dozen numbers from 13-24. Should any of those numbers come up on the next spin, you're a winner.

FIGURE 12

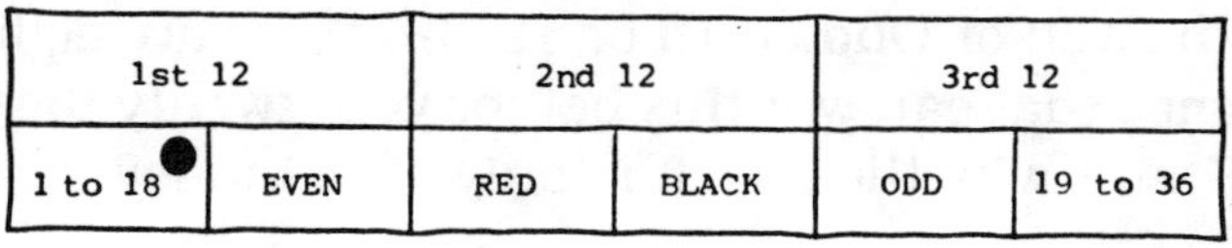

1st 12		2nd 12		3rd 12	
1 to 18 ●	EVEN	RED	BLACK	ODD	19 to 36

1-18 or 19-36

Some people think that since there are only two ways to make this bet, and since the payoff is even money, the player cannot possibly lose. They think that the player, at worst, should break even, winning one and losing the other. Unfortunately, those people forget that, whenever the outcome is 0 or 00, they lose both bets. Figure 12 shows a bet on 1-18. The chips do not have to be placed exactly as shown, as long as they are within the boundaries of the 1-18 bet.

Odd or Even

FIGURE 13

1st 12		2nd 12		3rd 12	
1 to 18	● EVEN	RED	BLACK	ODD	19 to 36

Here you have two choices, either of which pays even money. As long as the outcome of the next spin is an even number, your bet in Figure 13 would win. If the next outcome is an odd number or 0 or 00, you would lose.

Red or Black

FIGURE 14

1st 12		2nd 12		3rd 12	
1 to 18	EVEN	RED ●	BLACK	ODD	19 to 36

As with Even or Odd, 1-18 or 19-36, there are eighteen outcomes that can win this bet for you, twenty that can lose. That's why the payoff is only even money.

Column Bets

FIGURE 15

00	3	6	9	12	15	18	21	24	27	30	33	36	2–1
	2	5	8	11	14	17	20	23	26	29	32	35	● 2–1
0	1	4	7	10	13	16	19	22	25	28	31	34	2–1

Three choices, all of which pay two to one. Your bet in Figure 15 would win if any of the numbers in that column (2, 5, 8, 11, 14, 17, 20, 23, 26, 29, 32 or 35) come up on the next spin. Twelve numbers can win for you, the other twenty-six lose.

Of course, all these betting options can be mixed in any combination you desire. It's not uncommon to see people making one Two Number bet, a Four Number bet, a Column bet, and a Dozens bet all at the same time. But don't get carried away in the excitement of the moment. Sometimes people make so many different bets that they end up betting against themselves, putting themselves in a situation where, even if one of their numbers comes up, they can't possibly win enough to cover all the bets that lost.

To my mind, this game is for fun only. There are many systems on the market for winning at roulette and I've tried most of them, with varying degrees of failure. If you play Roulette you will see countless players with pads and pencils tracking the ebb and flow of each number in an attempt to outguess the ball and wheel. But the only way to win at this game is through out-and-out blind luck. If you are lucky enough to win, leave the table with your winnings. If you stay at the table, the generous advantage you give to the casino will soon grind you down.

Note: When betting on Even-Odd, Red-Black, or 1-18 and 19-36 in Atlantic City, the player has an additional option which is very favorable. This option is known as the *en prison* rule. If the player makes one of the even money bets listed above and 0 or 00 is the next outcome, the player has two choices.

1) The player can "imprison" the bet. This means the bet stays where it is. Then, if the bet wins on the next spin, the bet is returned to the player.

2) The player may surrender half the bet.

The *en prison* lowers the casino advantage to 2.7% on these bets, making these bets the best on the layout.

Basically, with the *en prison* option, you're given a second chance; you're given new life. Consequently, most people never surrender half their bet, preferring to exercise the *en prison* option. Don't be surprised if the croupier assumes that you will take the *en prison* option. Simply tell him you would prefer to surrender half your bet, if that is what you want to do.

If you choose to imprison your bet, the croupier will then mark your chips with a small plastic disc to differentiate them from the other bets on the layout. Then, the very next spin of the wheel will dictate whether that bet is returned to you or whether the casino collects it.

At least one casino in Atlantic City is using a Roulette wheel which contains only 0. 00 is not on the layout. This difference means that the casino's advantage on Inside Bets is reduced from 5.26% to approximately 2.3%. Obviously, if you want to play Roulette you should seek out these tables.

5
SLOT MACHINES

CONSIDER THIS PROPOSITION: You give me a dollar and I'll give you ninety cents. No deal, you say?

Okay, let me try another one: You give me $100 and I'll give you $90. Not just once. We'll make this exchange, your $100 or my $90, a hundred times each day. Still no deal? Well, let me sweeten the pot. You give me $100 and I'll give you $90 a hundred times each day for six days, and then on the seventh day of each week I'll give *you* $100 for every $80 you give me. Sound better? No, not really. If you were to agree to this proposition and try it for one week, I'd be $4000 ahead of you. I'd give you a total of $64,000 and you'd give me a total of $68,000. That is *not* a good deal.

Yet that is exactly how slot machines work. For every dollar put in them, they give back about ninety-five cents. That is, *some* of them give back ninety-five cents.

Some slot machines only return seventy or eighty cents for each dollar.

Would any intelligent person play a game in which the casino's advantage could be 20% or more? Remember Baccarat? A bet on banker's gives the casino an advantage of only 1.2%. Comparing a bet on banker's to playing slot machines, your chances of winning are nearly seventeen times greater at Baccarat! A bet on the Pass Line in Craps has over fourteen times greater chance of winning than a bet in a slot machine. So, the question becomes, why do people play slot machine?

Well, you know the answer as well as I do. People play slot machines because they're fun. Even though you know it's highly unlikely that you'll win, even though you know you're *donating* your money to the casino, you still play the metal monsters.

Since slot machines take up a large share of each casino's gaming area, I won't spend any time describing them. When you enter a casino, you can't possibly miss them. Most of them can be played for nickels, dimes, quarters, half-dollars and dollars. A few of the newer machines even require five dollars for each pull of the handle, while still others allow you to deposit from one to five coins, with each additional coin increasing your potential payoff.

To play a slot machine, you insert the coin or coins required and pull the lever usually found on the right side of the machine. Some machines have only three reels (also called columns or wheels), others have four or five. When you pull the handle, the reels spin and then stop one at a time. If you hit a winning combination, the machine spits your winnings into a metal catcher at the bottom of the machine, bells start ringing, lights flash, and sometimes sirens blare.

A list of all possible winning combinations can be

found on the machine's chest. Each reel normally contains twenty symbols: bars, bells, 7's, $'s, oranges, plums, and so forth. A machine might pay, for example, two coins if the first reel is a cherry, or five if the first *two* reels are cherries, or thirty coins if the *three* reels are all plums. The machines seldom make mistakes on payoffs, but make sure that you know all the winning combinations. More than one person has overlooked a winner that was not paid correctly.

Also, jackpots (the largest payoff given by the machine) are *not* normally paid entirely by the machine. If you hit a $200 jackpot the machine will only pay a small portion, the rest to be paid by an attendant. If you ever have the good fortune to hit a jackpot, *do not* play the machine again until *after* you have received your total prize. Many people assume that the machine has paid the total prize, so they play it again and cheat themselves out of hundreds of dollars. In addition, the attendant *must* see the winning combination before paying off. If you hit a jackpot *do not* leave the machine. Call for an attendant, scream for help, yell until you're hoarse, but do not leave the machine. The casino won't try to cheat you, but other gamblers might.

I once observed two women playing five machines each. Both would start at one slot machine, insert their coins, pull the handle and move on to the next machine with the reels of the first still spinning. Then each of them would start all over again, moving from machine to machine as though working on an assembly line in Detroit. This is not an uncommon sight, but what happened that day was unusual.

Both women were playing machines on the same side of the aisle. You guessed it. A machine in the middle hit the jackpot of $750. Can you guess what ensued? Right! Each woman claimed she'd been playing that machine.

The disagreement started politely enough, then escalated to a shoving and shouting match. Ever seen two forty-year-old women try to clobber each other? The confrontation was amusing to watch while it was verbal, dismal to see after one woman slapped the other. Both were hauled away by security guards. I hope that one of them collected that jackpot. I'm sure that both of them truly believed that the *other* woman was cheating.

Most of us fool around with slot machines in hope of hitting the jackpot. But what are your chances of this happening? Consider the following: If a slot machine has three reels, each with twenty symbols, there are 8,000 possible combination (20 x 20 x 20). And only *one* of those combinations will win the jackpot. If it is a dollar machine with a $750 jackpot, $8,000 could go into it before some lucky person wins the $750.

The next time you play a slot machine, try to remember the following:

1) If a machine has three reels, your odds of hitting the jackpot are 8,000 to 1.

2) If a machine has four reels, your odds of hitting the jackpot are 160,000 to 1.

3) If a machine has five reels, your odds of hitting the jackpot are 3,200,000 to 1.

Are the odds really that bad? Yes. But, you ask, does that mean I'd have to put $8,000 into a three-reel machine just to win $750? No. The reasons are twofold:

1) When you play a three-reel slot machine you don't know if your coin is the *first* to be inserted into that machine or the *7,999th* coin to be inserted.

2) If the machine is set to pay back 80% of the

money put into it, you should receive many small payoffs before hitting the jackpot. You still might have to pull the handle 8,000 times, but it wouldn't cost you $8,000.

Let's explore this further. I'll assume that you're playing a three-reel, dollar machine. The reason you're playing that particular machine is because you saw a sign in front of the casino which stated, "Our $1 Slots Pay 97%." You interpret the sign to mean that if you put in $100 you'll get back at least $97. Well, you could be right, you could be wrong. Your first coin could win the jackpot, your tenth coin could win the jackpot, any of your coins could win smaller payoffs, or perhaps *none* of your coins will win anything.

If this dollar machine really pays back 97%, out of every $8,000 put into it $7,760 will be returned to the players. In other words, the machine will only retain $240. But *whose* $240 will it retain? Yours? The next player's? Who knows? It may very well take $100 of your money and only give back $10. Then, for the very next person to play the machine, it may give back $30 for $1. There is no way to tell who the machine will pay. And it's even worse than I've described. The machine may keep $3,000 before returning *any* money. I once interviewed an attendant who had been watching one particular dollar machine for the entire four months of her tenure. During that time the machine had *never* paid a jackpot even though it had been in continuous use.

Instead of thinking about what a 97% machine might mean to *you*, think about what it means to the casino. If that machine is played 8,000 times each week (which is *very* possible), the casino will net $240 per week on that machine. That's $1,032 per month, $12,384 per year. If the casino had fifty such machines (again, *very* possible), the casino would net $619,200 each year! If the payoff rate was 90% instead of 97%, which is more than likely, it would net $2,064,000 per year. And if the payoff rate was 80% it would net $4,128,000 each year. Is it any wonder why casinos have so many slot machines? Would you like to have five or ten of them in your basement?

MONEY MANAGEMENT

In the introduction to this book, I suggested that no more than 20% of your gambling fund should be used as fun money. I now suggest that 20% of your 20% can be used for slot machines. If your fun money is $100, don't risk more than $20. I know that's not much money, but you can always play the nickel machines. Twenty dollars on nickel machines would give you 400 pulls of the handle, and the rate of payoff on the nickel machines is as good as any, the jackpots still in proportion to the more expensive machines. Whether you win $100 on a nickel machine or $2000 on a dollar machine, the ratio is the same. The dollar machine just costs a lot more to play.

Another suggestion: On some machines you can play from one to five coins on each pull, the payoff increasing for each coin; a one-coin jackpot might be $50, a two-coin jackpot $125, a three-coin jackpot $200, etc. On those machines it is in your best interests to play five coins on each pull.

Note: When playing the slots make sure that the machine accepts your coin or coins *before* you pull the handle. Sometimes, your coins can pass through the machine and drop in the metal catcher. I once hit a jackpot while playing a three-coin machine. Unfortunately, only one of my three coins had been accepted by the machine, but I hadn't noticed. My jackpot paid at the one-coin rate of $100. Had all three of my coins been accepted, the payoff would have been $500! My lack of attention cost me $400.

Have fun with slot machines. Just don't expect to win any money.

6

KENO

AS AN EXPERIMENT, I once asked ten random gamblers to describe the game of Keno. All ten of those people started by saying that Keno was similar to Bingo. Both are played with numbered cards and with ping pong balls drawn from a machine. Bingo has 75 numbers. Keno has 80 numbers. But Bingo and Keno are *not* similar.

In Bingo, numbers are drawn until someone wins. If it takes 65 numbers to produce a winner, the 65 numbers are drawn. There is a winner in every game.

In Keno, only *20* numbers are drawn. In Keno, it is quite possible that a game will have *no* winner.

To play Keno, you must first obtain a Keno card (ticket). You'll find these at the Keno counter, in the Keno lounge, and in all the casino's bars and restaurants. The tickets are free and easily found. You then select from one to fifteen of your favorite numbers. If some or all of

MARK PRICE HERE

$1.00

1	2	3	4	5	6	7	8	9	10
11	12	13	14	15	16	17	18	19	20
21	22	23	24	25	26	27	28	29	30
31	32	33	34	35	36	37	38	39	40
$50,000.00 AGGREGATE									
41	42	43	44	45	46	47	48	49	50
51	52	53	54	55	56	57	58	59	60
61	62	63	64	65	66	67	68	69	70
71	72	73	74	75	76	77	78	79	80

8/

FIGURE 1

your numbers are drawn from the Keno blower in the next game, you could win from $1 to $50,000. Figure 1 shows a Keno ticket played for $1 with eight numbers selected. In addition to checking the numbers you desire, you must also indicate on the ticket how many numbers you're playing and how much money you're wagering.

After filling out the ticket you take it to the Keno counter, pay your wager, and receive an authorized copy of your ticket with the game number noted in the upper right corner.

Figure 2 shows what your authorized copy will look like. If you're sitting in a bar or restaurant, you can also have a Keno girl take your ticket and money to the Keno counter. But if the Keno girl does not get your ticket to the counter in time for the next game, or if she makes a

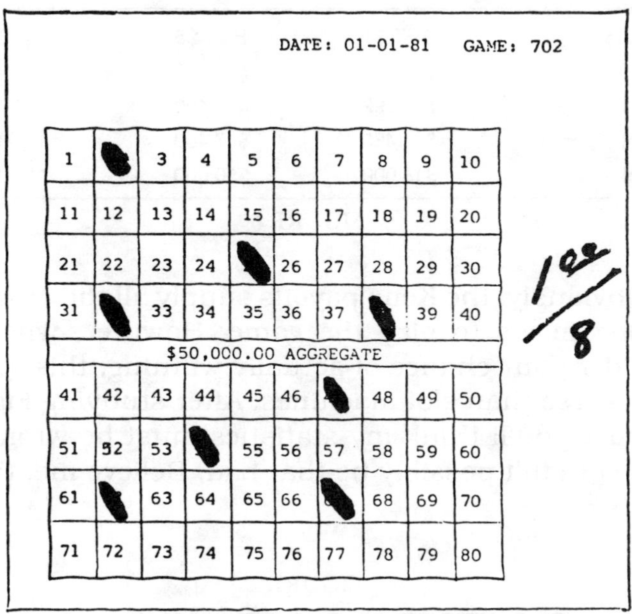

FIGURE 2

mistake of some kind, the casino is not responsible for her.

Once you've paid for your ticket and received your authorized copy, there's nothing for you to do but sit back and relax. You have no control over the game. Eighty ping pong balls will decide your fate.

As the numbers are drawn from the Keno blower they are flashed onto Keno boards which are located throughout the casino. Whether you win anything depends on how many of your selected numbers are drawn. For your eight number ticket, typical payoffs are shown in Figure 3.

If six of your numbers were drawn, you would win $92 for your $1 bet. Sound good? Had all eight of your numbers been drawn, you would win $18,000 for your $1 bet. Sound even better?

CATCH	BET $1	BET $5	BET $20
5 WIN	$ 9	$ 45	$ 180
6 WIN	$ 92	$ 460	$ 1,840
7 WIN	$ 1,480	$ 7,400	$29,600
8 WIN	$18,000	$50,000	$50,000

FIGURE 3

Obviously, the Keno payoffs supply all the attraction anyone needs to play the game. However, when you consider your chance of actually winning, this game is even worse than slot machines. After studying Figure 4 I'm sure you'll think my statistics must be wrong, the odds couldn't possibly be that bad. Believe me, the *are* that bad!

FIGURE 4

IF YOU SELECT	THE ODDS OF ALL YOUR NUMBERS BEING DRAWN ARE
1	4-1
2	17-1
3	72-1
4	326-1
5	1,550-1
6	7,755-1
7	40,843-1
8	230,230-1
9	1,381,380-1
10	8,909,900-1
11	62,369,300-1
12	478,370,000-1
13	4,066,145,000-1
14	38,911,000,000-1
15	428,027,820,000-1

No, you didn't read it wrong. If you select ten numbers on your Keno ticket, the chance of all ten numbers being drawn is roughly one in nine million. If you select fifteen numbers, the chance of all fifteen being drawn is one in slightly over four hundred billion.

The casino's advantage is difficult to determine in this game, but the smallest advantage is about 25% on a one-number ticket. And the casino's advantage could run as high as 99.999999999%!

However, there is always the chance that your ten-number ticket is the one out of nine million. There is also the chance that six of your ten numbers might be drawn, or nine of your ten. Don't count on it. The odds are still so bad that you'd have a better chance of striking oil in your back yard. If you want to play a ten-number ticket nine million times in an effort to win $50,000, perhaps I can interest you in Colorado pine cones which I'm willing to sell for only $5,000 each.

If your ticket does win anything, you can collect your winnings at the Keno counter or have the Keno girl make the trip for you. Winning tickets *must be* collected before the start of the next game.

Also, please note in Figures 1 and 2 the mid-ticket message: $50,000 *AGGREGATE*. That means that the total maximum payoff for all winners in any one game is $50,00. If there is more than one winner in a single game, the total payoff to *all* winners cannot exceed $50,000. So just because you get a $50,000 winner does not mean you will collect $50,000.

MONEY MANAGEMENT

If your vacation is for three days and two nights, you'll probably eat eight meals at your hotel casino. During the time required to eat each meal, you could play three games of Keno. At $1 per game, that's $24. No, I'm not suggesting that you risk $24 on Keno. All I'm saying is that you *could* risk $24. Personally, I think one game per meal is ideal. That's only $8. Any more than that is lunacy. You can't protect your money in games where the casino has *at least* a 25% advantage over the player.

7

PAI GOW POKER

PICTURE THIS: You've just arrived at a casino that you've never before visited. You notice a small group of people clustered around a table in one of the Blackjack pits. You approach the group to see why everyone in the crowd seems to be studying the action taking place on the table. The players at the table consist of five Orientals and one Caucasian. Instead of cards, you see these plastic things on the table which resemble dominoes. No one in the crowd seems to have the slightest understanding of what is happening. The five Orientals at the table seem to be having fun, but the lone Caucasian appears to be slightly perplexed. You look up and notice a sign which announces that the game you are watching is called "Pai Gow".

Okay, now that you have the picture, remember this: Do not even attempt to play this game! Those plastic things that look like dominoes are actually the equivalent of Chinese playing cards. The figures which make them appear to be dominoes are actually Chinese numbers. So, unless you can read Chinese numbers, it is virtually impossible for you to play this game. This is why the five Orientals at the table seem to be having fun, but the lone Caucasian is lost, and no one watching the game can figure out what is happening. Could you play Blackjack if the playing cards contained no numbers or figures? Of course not. So why try to play a game in which you are literally blind?

All of the above is the bad news. Here is the good news. Same scenario; You are walking through a new casino and you see these people grouped around a Blackjack table. At the table are seated two Orientals and four players who are not Oriental. There are playing cards distributed in front of each player, but it is obvious that the game is not Blackjack. The dealer appears to be performing some sort of ceremony with a canister of dice. You say to yourself: Oh, oh, this must be another one of those crazy games which can only be played by people with mysterious and special knowledge. Well, my friend, you are wrong, wrong, wrong!

The game you are now observing is called Pai Gow *Poker*. Please note that the first game I talked about was called Pai Gow, and this game is called Pai Gow *Poker*. Again, unless you can read Chinese numbers, do not even think about playing Pai Gow. But, please make every attempt during your next visit to play Pai Gow Poker, because it is an easy game to learn and a fun game to play, particularly if you find the pace of the normal games like Blackjack and Craps to be too hectic.

Pai Gow Poker is a game which combines elements of the ancient Chinese game of pai Gow, and the American game of Poker. So, if you have ever played Poker at any level, including Video Poker, you should be able to play Pai Gow Poker. So long as you have a basic understanding of the ranking of winning hands in Poker, you can play this game.

Let's assume you decide to sit in for a few games. Here's what happens: First, you must make a wager. At most tables, the minimum is ten dollars, though you may find less expensive stakes if you're visiting during the week. You may think that the ten dollar minimum seems a tad steep for your taste, but don't worry; in the time it takes to play one hand of Pai Gow Poker, you could have played 5-7 hands of Blackjack. As I stated earlier, this game has a nice pace to it, and is not played with the frenzy of some of the other games. As is the case with blackjack, there will be a small circular or rectangular area on the felt in which you should place the chips for your wager.

The dealer shuffles the cards and deals seven hands consisting of seven cards each, in piles directly in front of her. The players don't get the cards yet. (I'll assume the dealer is female, so when I say "she", I am referring to the dealer.) She starts dealing from her left, makes seven piles working to her right, then reverses her action, moving from right to left for the second card in the pile, then left to right again, etc. until each pile has exactly seven cards. She then counts the cards left in her hand to make sure that she has the correct number of cards remaining. You quickly multiply in your head that seven piles of seven cards each should be a total of 49 cards dealt, which means that she should have 3 cards left out of a single deck of 52 cards, but you are wrong. This playing deck consists of the 52 regular cards, plus one joker, so when the dealer counts the cards remaining in her hand she should find four.

The next step is that the dealer picks up a small cup, usually metal, and shakes it to mix up the three dice contained inside. She then flips the cup over, reveals the dice, and counts the total of them. The die, by the way, look like the same dice used at Craps, except that they are smaller, and each contains the numbers 1 to 6, so that the total of the three dice could be any number from 3 to 18. The total of the dice is what determines which player is to receive the first hand. For, you see, if the piles of cards were distributed in the same order on every hand, the dealer may at times be accused of stacking the deck in her favor. But since the dice determine which hand she will be playing, there is no way for her to predetermine which hand to stack.

The dealer's position is counted as number 1, number 8, or number 15, depending on the total of dice. That is, the *Banker's* position is counted as number 1, 8, or 15, but since the dealer is almost always the Banker, just think of it that way, and I'll explain the difference later.

Let's assume that the total of the dice was 4. The dealer counts herself as one, the first person to her right as two, the second person as three, and the third person as four. So the third person from her right is given the first hand, which is the first stack on her right, and then the rest of the piles are passed out to player number five, number, six, number seven, the dealer, then players number two and three. If this sounds a little confusing, don't worry about it. You have no control over the distribution of the hands. The important issue at this point is that all that stuff, that ritual that looked so mysterious when you were watching the people play this game is not so mysterious, after all. Also, here is a diagram that may help you understand.

Player	Player	Player	Player	Player	Player
7	6	5	4	3	2
14	13	12	11	10	9

Dealer
1
8
15

Keeping this chart in mind, you can see that if the total number from the dice were 4, then the player at the number 4 position would receive the first hand, and the player at position number 3 would receive the last hand. If the total dice number came to 13, then the player at position number 13 (which is also position number 6) would receive the first hand, and the player at position number 12 would receive the last hand. The only time the dealer would receive the last hand would be if the dice total 2, 9, or 16. I hope this makes sense to you, but if it doesn't this will not effect your ability to play the game.

Now you have seven cards in front of you, placed there in a nice, neat stack by the dealer. Your next step is to pick them up, look at them, and hope that you can make some sort of Poker hand out of them, Not just one Poker hand, but two. You are going to make up what you can think of as your highest Poker hand, and your second highest Poker hand. All of the other players at the table, plus the dealer, are going to do the same. The object of the game is for your first highest Poker hand to be higher than the dealer's first highest hand, and also for your second highest hand to be higher than the dealer's second highest hand. Some people find it more convenient to think of these two hands as a high hand and a low hand, but since we don't really want a low hand, I like to think of it as my best hand and my second best hand.

The ranking of hand is basically the same as in regular Poker; Five Aces, Royal Flush, Straight Flush, Four of a Kind, Full House, Flush, Straight, Three of a Kind, Two Pair, One Pair, and High Card. Those of you who play poker regularly may now be saying, wait a minute, you can't have a hand of Five Aces unless you have a wild card. And while we are not playing with any truly "wild" cards, you may recall that we are playing with one Joker in the deck. This Joker, while not being completely "wild", can be used with Aces, Straights, and Flushes. In other words, if you have an Ace and a Joker, you really have two Aces. If you have three Aces and a Joker, you really have two Aces. If you have three Aces and a Joker, you really have four Aces. Should you have Eight, Nine, Ten, Jack, and Joker, you have a Straight. A hand consisting of Seven, Eight, Ten, Jack, and Joker, would also be a straight. If you had four spades and the Joker, you have a flush. If you have a pair of Queens and a pair of Kings, plus a Joker, you have a pair of Queens and a pair of Kings, and the Joker is worthless to this hand.

Again, we are going to make two Poker hands out of the seven cards you are now holding. Our best hand will consist of five cards and our second best hand will only consist of two cards. Since most Poker hands consist of five cards, this should not be difficult for us. We simply look at the seven cards, and separate the five which make the best poker hand. This then leaves us with two cards which we can utilize as our second best hand. The ranking of the two-card hand is slightly different merely because it only contains two cards; subsequently the two card hand cannot contain a straight, a flush, or any other ranking except for high card or a pair. Sounds easy enough, right? Well, it is a little more complicated than that because you must keep in mind that we want to beat both the dealer's best and second best hands. In fact, the only time we win is when we beat *both* of the dealers' hands. What? You mean I gotta beat both of them? Yes, that's what I'm saying, and I know that sounds pretty tough, but the news gets better. On those occasions when we only beat *one* of the dealer's hands, we lose nothing, we gain nothing, we have a draw and no money exchanges hands. And in order for the dealer to collect *our* money, the dealer must either beat or tie both of our hands. Yes, the dealer wins ties. But don't concern yourself too much with the news that the dealer wins ties, because this almost never happens.

The bottom line here, as they say in the business world, is that you can play a lot of hands without either gaining or losing a lot of money and have a very good time while doing it. This is because if you play your cards properly you won't find many instances of the dealer beating you senseless unless your luck is simply very bad. And the reason for this is that unless we have cards which will make us two good hands, we always play for the tie. Yes, I know this sounds defensive, but it is also smart.

Now, one last piece of information you must have in order to play this game. Your best hand, the one which is made up of five cards, *must* be higher than your second best hand. This only makes sense, but this is also where a lot of people end up making mistakes, and should you make the mistake of arranging your cards so that your second best hand is higher in ranking than your best hand, you lose automatically. P.S. You also lose automatically if you mistakenly place only three or four cards in your highest hand, or make any arrangement that does not consist of five cards and two cards.

Let's see if we can make sense out of all of this. You sit down, make a bet of ten dollars, the dealer shuffles, the dealer makes seven little piles in front of her consisting of seven cards each, the dealer shakes the dice, the total of the dice is 9, so the player all the way over at the end of the table (third base in Blackjack lingo) receives the first hand, and the player at position number 15, which is the dealer, gets the last pile of cards.

Your hand consists of the following: Ace of spades, Queen of spades, Joker, Nine of diamonds, Ten of diamonds, Queen of clubs, and King of spades. Get out a deck of cards and deal yourself this exact hand and you'll find this example easier to follow. Obviously, this is not a great hand, but we may be able to get out of it with a tie. We have no Flush, or Straight, so we are only looking at Pairs. Most people, upon receiving these cards, would immediately arrange their two hand like this:

Highest hand: A/S, J, Q/S, Q/C, K/S

Second highest: 9/D, 10D

This means that their best hand is a pair of aces (remember that the Joker is another Ace), a pair of Queens, and the leftover King. The second best hand is simply the other two leftover cards which did not help the high hand, the Nine and Ten of diamonds. Two pair is not a bad hand, and if you consider the ranking of hands, the dealer would have to have three of a kind or better to beat our two pair for the best hand. So let's assume for a moment that two pair could very well beat the dealer's best hand. Now let's think about the chances we left for our second best hand. Remember, just because it is the second best does not mean that we can merely throw all of our "junk" into this hand and hope for the best. You must think in terms of making the two best hands possible. Bearing this in mind, how else could we play this exact hand and improve our chances of winning: A) at least one of the hands, or B) both hands?

Well, how about if we made this change:

Highest hand: A/S, J, Q/S, Q/C, 9/D

Second highest: K/S, 10D

Now we are playing a pair of Aces plus trash for the high hand, and a pair of Queens for the second highest. The thinking here is that while our pair of Aces may not win for high, our pair of Queens will almost assuredly win for the second highest and we'll at least guarantee ourselves a tie on this hand. And now for those of you who thought I had overlooked one of our best possibilities, what if we remembered that our Joker can be used as the fifth card if we have four towards a Straight or Flush, and thus arranged our cards like this:

Highest hand: 9/D, 10/D, J, Q/C, K/S

Second Highest: A/S, Q/S

A Straight for the best hand is quite powerful, almost a certainty to beat the dealer's high hand, and the Ace and Queen we have leftover for the second best hand is also very playable. Arranging the cards in this manner provides us with nearly a "lock" for best, and a good shot at also winning second best.

Always remember that we want to arrange our cards so that we have a chance of winning at least one of the hands. I am sure that some of my readers will take the "macho" approach, think that playing for a tie is like kissing their sister, and put all their high cards in the best hand. The rest of us, however, will play more conservatively, keep more of our money, and play longer on less money even when we don't get decent cards.

Another example: You are dealt the Deuce of clubs,

the Four of hearts, the Six of hearts, the Seven of diamonds, the Seven of hearts, the Eight of diamonds, and the Nine of clubs. How do you arrange your hand? what about this:

Highest hand: 2/C, 4/H, 6/H, 8/D, 9/C

Second highest: 7/D, 7/H

Obviously, the person who would arrange their hand in this manner is thinking that the trash is worthless, so why not put it in the high hand and save the pair of sevens for the second best hand. The logic is all right, but the result is that this person will lose their bet because their second best hand carries a higher ranking than their best hand, which is definitely against the rules. This person has no choice but to arrange this hand thusly:

Highest hand: 7/D, 7/H, 2/C, 4/H, 6/H

Second highest: 8/D, 9/C

Yes, I know that this hand appears to have no chance for either hand, but strange things happen. Every once in a while, the dealer is dealt a hand that contains Cow Pie. Cow Pie is just the opposite of Pai Gow, and kind of rhymes, so some player some time in history decided the term Cow Pie was appropriate for describing a dealer hand which contains absolutely nothing; a hand even worse than the hand I described immediately before this paragraph. So even when you receive terrible cards, do not despair. As with other games of chance, you can sometimes win with terrible cards and lose with fantastic cards.

Let's consider one more hand and contemplate our options. You receive the Ace of spades, the 9 of spades, the Jack of spades, the 10 of diamonds, the Joker, the 7 of spades, and the 3 of spades. You immediately recognize that you have a very nice spade Flush and arrange your hands like this:

Highest hand: A/S, J/S, 9/S, 3/S

Second highest: 10/D, J

Granted, you're excited to have the nice flush, but you've just turned a great hand into one which will probably end up with a tie at best. Note that the highest card in your second hand is a 10. Remember that the Joker by itself is a worthless card. Think about what your options are! Why waste that Ace in your highest hand when you could put it to better use in your second highest hand? Why not play the hand like this:

Highest hand: J/S, 9/S, 7/S, 3/S, J

Second highest: A/S, 10/D

Now you still have a Flush (recall that the Joker can be the fifth card in a Straight or Flush) for the best hand, and the Ace puts you in better shape for the second hand. Also, did you notice that this hand also contains a Straight, and could be arranged like this:

Highest hand: J/S, 10/D, 9/S, J, 7/S

Second highest: A/S, 3/S

However, why would anyone in their right mind want to play a Straight for high with an Ace, Three for second best, when they could have a flush for high with an Ace, 10 for second?

Hopefully, these examples have shown some of the choices you'll need to make in order to play this game. You will not be rushed for them, so think twice about your selections.

At any rate, let's assume your hand was the one we just finished talking about, with the spade Flush for high and the Ace, 10 for second best. Here's what happens next; First you place the best (five card hand) in a little rectangular box drawn on the table felt which usually says "highest". The second best (two card hand) goes into another box outlined on the table immediately adjacent to the box for the highest hand. You weren't supposed to look at the cards of the other players when they picked them up, but I always try to get a glimpse if possible. The casino doesn't want any players combining cards for better hands, or even discussing their individual hands, but don't worry too much about this aspect of the game unless someone infers that you should not try to stretch the rules.

Once all the players have their hands aligned in the boxes on the table, the dealer reveals all seven of the cards dealt to her. That's right, up to now she has been waiting for the players to do their thing, and now it's her turn. She turns over her cards, and you hope to see Cow Pie, but this time you are disappointed. Let's assume the dealer has a hand like this: Ten of hearts, Ten of clubs, Five of clubs, Five of diamonds, Jack of spades, Seven of diamonds, and Three of hearts. There is no doubt about what the dealer is going to do with this hand. It will be played like this:

Highest hand: 10/H, 10/C, J/S, 7/D, 3/H

Second highest: 5/C, 5/D

The reason the dealer plays in this manner is logical if you think about it. The dealer is playing for the tie, hoping that while she will probably lose with only one pair in her high hand, she will win most of the second best hands with a low pair. The dealer is playing not to lose. Remember that you are only playing against the dealer, but the dealer is playing against the entire table. She could arrange her hand so that it contained the two pair for the best hand and the Jack, 7 for second best, but then she would lose to everyone at the table who had three of a kind or better for best hand, and a Queen or better for second best.

The next step is that the dealer exposes the hands of the players, starting at third base and working backwards (counter clockwise) around to first base. All hands are compared to the dealer's hands, cards and bets for hands that are losers are collected as she works her way around the table, ties and winners are left out until she is done, then settled as required.

And then another hand begins.

Now, does that sound all that difficult? Of course not. The game moves at a nice pace, you're not at all rushed, you do not win or lose on every hand because of the ties which occur, and there is probably not a pit boss standing over your shoulder. So, as I concluded after learning how to play this game, this is a game which everyone should play. But, I should mention some other details before we finish up on this topic.

First, when you lose your bet, it is gone. However, when you win a bet, a 5% commission is collected — which is something similar to Bacarrat. Actually, the 5% is not collected immediately. Instead, the dealer keeps track of your commissions payable by placing little markers in little boxes which correspond to each player at the table. These markers must be collected before you can leave the table, and are also collected when there is a change of dealers.

Even though you actually only win $9.50 for every $10.00 bet, I still think this is a good game to play. As you can figure for yourself, your disadvantage is precisely the 5% commission you pay only on winning wagers. And while a 5% disadvantage means you have better odds at other games, Pai Gow Poker is every bit as fun as Roulette, Keno, or Slot Machines and can provide a rest from the frenzy of Blackjack or Craps without creating exposure to truly ridiculous odds like those associated with Roulette, Keno, etc.

Banker. Remember when I mentioned the Banker early on in this chapter? I said that since the dealer is ordinarily the Banker, I would leave this for the end. Well, this is the end, so here's what you need to know about the Banker.

First, you, yes you, can be the Banker should you desire. Simply let the dealer know that you want to be the Banker and she will be sure to accommodate you. Being the Banker means that you are the person who either collects or pays off all of the players at the table depending upon whether your hands are better or worse than theirs. In other words, you replace the dealer and everyone is playing against you.

However, being the Banker does not relieve you of the problem of beating the dealer. When a player is also the Banker, the first thing that happens is that the dealer compares her hand with the Banker's hand. She wins, loses, or ties, just like the players. The dealer then exposes all the rest of the hands, determines whether they win or lose when compared to the Banker's hand, then assists the Banker in either collecting or paying off bets. Yes, the house still collects the 5% commission on winning wagers.

Other than wanting to seem important, there is a legitimate reason for being the Banker. The Banker wins all ties. So if you lose one hand and tie the other, you lose your wager.

I have never been the Banker, even though winning all ties does improve the odds against me in this game, for the simple reason that I play this game to relax between serious gambling sessions at Blackjack, my game of choice. Why would I want to make myself tense by worrying about whether I can beat everyone at the table? Should you choose to be the Banker, I suggest you study the betting habits of the other players at the table. If the other players are wagering more than you can collectively afford to pay off, don't become the Banker.

Pai Gow Poker is a game you should try to play. Do it!!

8

AMERICAN POKER/CASINO STYLE

IF YOU HAVE ABSOLUTELY NO KNOWLEDGE of how to play Poker, please purchase a book which will teach you the basics. It is not my intent in this chapter to help make you a great Poker player, or even a better Poker player. The purpose of this chapter is to explain the differences between how Poker is played in Nevada and how it is played in the normal, friendly (alright, sometimes maybe not so friendly) game you are accustomed to playing in New York, Nebraska,wherever you happen to live. I am discussing the Nevada brand of Poker, because Poker is not currently played in Atlantic City.

The best reason for playing Poker in a casino is that unlike the other casino games, you are not competing against the house. You are now testing your skill and luck against other people just like yourself. No one has you at a fixed percentage disadvantage.

Yet, even though my reason as stated above is true, I firmly believe that the real reason people enjoy Casino Style Poker is that it gives them a chance to test their skill against some of the best Poker players in the world. You are not playing against your Uncle Fred, who couldn't care less if he loses,your Aunt Mildred, who still can't remember that she should not fold when all her cards are of the same suit,your friend Jerry, who can be bluffed consistently by anyone who raises more than a quarter. You will now be playing with people who, for the most part, really know how to play. Granted, I've seen players who couldn't pass muster in a penny ante game, let alone a Vegas casino, but these folks are the exception and not the rule. Whether you decide to play in a $1-$3 game,a "no limit" game, the vast majority of the players at your table will be better than the people you play against at home.

For years, I avoided playing Poker at the casinos because I had heard from a number of people that I would be fleeced immediately by the locals regardless of my level of skill. The local players, the story went, had played with each other for years, had developed secret signs to tell each other what they were holding, and would gang up on all the "tourists". Were this true, a person really could be trounced severely regardless of skill level. However, once I decided to play, I found that these stories were unfounded. Granted, you may sit in at a game somewhere and encounter a few sharpies playing as a team, but that would definitely be the exception and not the rule. It is true, nonetheless, that I have sat in on a number of games where virtually all of the other players seemed to know each other. At first I thought this was a great disadvantage, because while they had only to figure out one style of play (mine), I had to figure out the style of play of each person at the table.

Fortunately, I finally figured out that the converse could also be true: I had them at a disadvantage because none of the knew *my* style.

On the low end, most poker games will fall into the $1-$3 category. On the high end, the sky is the limit. Obviously, you should only play in games you can tolerate financially. No matter how good you think you are, I wouldn't suggest that you tackle the top seven finishers in last years World Series of Poker until you've tested your skill at a lower level.

Here are the major differences between the Poker you play at home, and the way it's done in the casinos.

TYPES OF GAMES PLAYED

That's right, you will not find any "wild card" games being dealt in the casinos. The fare is basic. Seven Card Stud (both high, low, and high-low split), Texas Hold'em (high only), Omaha (high, and high-low split), and Five Card Draw. If you don't know how to play Seven Card Stud or Five Card Draw, buy a book about Poker. Texas Hold'em commonly known as Hold'em, is probably the most popular game as I write this.

Hold'em is a game which accommodates a large number of players, because few cards are used. Each player receives two cards down, you bet, there is a "flop" of three cards in the center of the table. These three cards are played just as though they were actually in your hand. Of course, they can be used by everyone else, too. You bet, there is another flop of one card, you bet, there is a final flop of one card, you bet, and someone wins. If you stay for all the cards, you'll have two in your hand, and five "common" flop cards out in the middle of the table. You must use the two cards in your hand and three of the cards from the flop to make up your five-card hand.

Omaha is similar to Hold'em. Everyone receives four cards down instead of two. The flop is the same; three, one, and one. You bet between all the intervals. This is usually a high-low split game. And even though you have four cards in your possession, and a total of nine cards when the "common" cards are included, you can only play five at a time. In addition, you can only play two from your hand. That's right, you *must* play two from your hand and three from the common cards laying out there in the center of the table. Yes, you can play two of your four cards for low and the other two for high,you can play the same two,any combination of the four cards taken two at a time, but you must play two from your hand. And another thing: there is usually no split unless someone has at least an Eightlower for the low hand. That's correct, if no one has at least an Eight for low the entire pot goes to the high Poker hand. Yes, this makes for a very interesting game.

NUMBER OF PLAYERS

It is not at all uncommon for a table to seat eight to ten players. Yes, I know that you can't play Seven Card Stud with eight players because 7 x 8 = 56. However, it's done in the casinos all the time. The reason? There is seldom a hand when all 52 cards are used. Invariably, at least two or three players drop after seeing their first few cards. In the case of Hold'em and Omaha, ten players is more the rule than exception. With Hold'em, the size of the table is the only reason not to have thirteen, sixteen, or, for that matter, twenty-two players. If the table was made that large, however, the players at each end would need opera glasses to see the cards at the other end of the felt.

THE DEALER

When you're playing with your friends, relatives,whomever, you each take turns shuffling and dealing the cards. In the casino game, the casino provides a person to do that for you. Yes, this prevents some card shark from stacking a deck, and is intended to keep the game honest and above board. Dealers typically rotate every twenty to thirty minutes. In addition to dealing the cards, they provide chips when you need to purchase them, watch the pot to make sure that all the players are contributing as they should, and announce the winning hands. The dealer is also there to answer any questions you may have, to explain all the basic rules, and settle any minor disputes. Do not hesitate to ask the dealer questions, no matter how busy they appear to be. It would be very ignorant to play in a game if you're not clear on the rules. For his or her services, the dealer is compensated by the casino and the tips donated by the players. In games where the pot is small, the tip should be at least a quarter or half-dollar. When you win a good size pot, tip a dollar or more. Or, don't tip at all if you don't like the dealer. It's up to you. I think it is interesting to note that the dealers I've interviewed indicate they usually make better tips in the small and medium size games. One told me the story of the hand he dealt which ended with a pot of over $30,000. His tip: nothing.

FIXED BETTING PROCEDURES

At home, if you're playing a game in which the high hand wins, the first bettor will usually be the person with the highest card showing. In the casino, the first bettor will normally be the person with the *lowest* card showing. For games in which there is no card showing, like Hold 'em, the first bettor is the person who is seated left of the "button". Never heard of a button? It's simply a small disc which rotates around the table, moving one player at a time after each game, so that the initial bettor is different every game. Another way to think of it is that the button identifies the "pretend" dealer. Since the deal does not rotate, the button does.

The first bet is always a fixed wager, whether it is a quarter, a dollar,several dollars. Of course this depends on the level of the game you are playing. This first bet is known as the "blind forced" bet, because the person on the hotseat (the first bettor) *must* make this wager. This person does not have the option of folding should he or she not appreciate the first cards dealt to them. The blind bet is always for a fixed amount, say $1 in a $1-$4 game. No more, no less. In some games, there are two blinds or forced bets. The first bettor must make, say, a $1 wager, the next person must make, say, a $2 wager; again, no more, no less. And, finally, there is another type of blind which is called a "live" blind. This describes a situation where everyone who stays in the game calls the bet of the blind, but no one raises. Should this happen, the blind then has the opportunity to raise himself.

After the blind or forced betting has taken place, the rest of the betting must also follow a pattern. In a $1-$3 game of Stud, for example, you may not be able to bet $3 until the last round of cards has been dealt.

If you see a game advertised as $1-$3-$6, this would mean that a wager of $6 is allowed on the final betting round.

There is an ante in some games, none in others.

When there is an ante, it is usually fairly small, like a quarter in a $1-$3 game.

Raise, raise, raise. That's correct, in most games the number of raises is limited to three. But, unlike most home games, when there are only two players remaining in the pot, there is no limit to the number of raises allowed. If two of you decide you have a hand that just simply cannot lose, then you can raise each other until there is no money left.

Wanna get down and dirty in a completely legitimate manner? Then check and raise. Though this is very uncommon in most home games, it's allowed in virtually every casino poker room I've ever seen. Remember, you're playing with the "big" boys now.

HOUSE TAKE

Did you think the casino was providing this poker room just so the dealers could make money? At the casino, this is called the "rake". I suppose it got the name from the manner in which the dealer's shove or rake the chips into the box under the table.

The size of the rake varies from game to game, so here are some typical examples.

Betting Limit	% of Rake	W/Maximum of
$1-$3	10	$3.00
$3-$6	5	$2.50
$1-$2-$4	10	$3.50
$1-$4-$8	5	$2.00

The rake will generally be more in Stud, less in Hold'em. This is because less hands are dealt per hour in Stud, and Hold'em typically has higher pots, so the casino collects the maximum more often. The amount of the rake, plus a list of the games and some of the basic rules is always listed near the entrance to any poker room. Just look for it. If you fail to look, just ask the dealer.

MINIMUM BUY-IN

You can't sit down to play unless you have at least X number of dollars in chips. The amount of the buy-in is listed on the same board that tells you the rake, etc. In a typical $1-$3 game, the buy-in would be at least $20.

Once the game has begun, the table stakes rule applies; if you run out of chips you can only play for that portion of the pot to which you contributed. However, most places will allow you to purchase additional chips providing that your money is already on the table. In other words, you buy-in for $20. You place your $20 worth of chips on top of another $30.00 in cash. The cash counts as chips being on the table so you can buy more chips at any time during a game.

If you don't already have cash on the table, you cannot go into your pocket, billfold,purse during a game. Of course, you can always purchase more chips between games.

BURN CARDS

This is another way of keeping the game honest. It is possible for players to mark the cards as the game is being played. If a player does this, then they could identify the top card on the deck. To prevent this, the dealer shuffles, someone cuts, and then the dealer burns a card before beginning the first round, and before beginning each subsequent round.

PLACING OF CHIPS IN THE POT

At home, when you call a bet, or raise, you toss your chips into the middle of the pile accumulating in the middle of the table. In the Poker Room at the casino, you do it a little differently. Instead of sending the chips to the middle of the table, you slide them out slightly in front of your playing position. Instead of sliding your chips out in a stack, you slide them out so that they are slightly spread apart. When you raise, you slide out two rows of bets; one to call, the other to raise. Do it this way, and you'll make life much easier for the dealer and your fellow players. If the chips of each player are distributed as I indicate, a simple glance around the table will tell you who is staying, raising, etc. After the betting is finished for each round, the dealer then scrapes all the chips into one big pile in the middle of the table.

If you keep heaving your chips into the pile, people like me might very well wonder if you really tossed six chips and not five. Get my drift?

Should you desire to fold, toss your cards into the middle of the table. Yes, now it's okay to toss.

CARDS PLAY

There is no need for you to declare the value or ranking of your hand. The dealer will read your cards and determine whether you have a winning hand. You should know the ranking of your hand, so that you recognize if the dealer makes an error, but the cards play themselves; just turn them over and hope you have the best hand.

CONSERVATIVE PLAY

If you're like me, and you're playing at home, and the game is of the nickel-dime-quarter variety, you never drop out of a hand which has even the most remote of possibilities. Consequently, it is not unusual to have seven players contending for a pot after the last round of betting. Obviously, this is something you will rarely, if ever, see in a Casino Poker Room. In a Stud game consisting of eight players, the final round will normally see no more than two to four players.

You must decide for yourself how to play your cards. But if you play every hand which contains only marginal possibilities, you will be swallowed alive. If, on the other hand, you are accustomed to playing only those hands which offer sound possibilities, you will fit right in.

SPEED OF PLAY

This is the first thing I noticed when I began playing Casino Style Poker. The game moves a lot faster than any I had experienced previously. There is not much idle chitchat between players. The dealer makes every attempt to keep the game moving along. The players, overall, are smarter, and take less time to make decisions. I don't mean to imply that any particular game is all business. There is conversation among the players and the dealers. There is joking and wise comments. But the pace is quicker.

Those are the differences which you need to be aware of before you try a Poker Room. The actual playing of the hands still depends on the style, intelligence,experience of the individual player. You can play Stud for hours and never see a winning hand better than three of a kind, then lose with a Straight Flush. You can stay in a game of Hold'em hoping to fill a Flush and accidentally win with a Queen High because everyone else folds. You can stay in a game of Omaha simply because no one else is betting like they have anything, and either get massacred or win with a small pair. It's still Poker. You're playing in a different environment, but it's still Poker.

For those of you who are still too timid to sit in at a Casino Poker Room, you can still try the Video Poker machines. No one will notice your mistakes. You can play many more hands per hour. Your odds of winning are as bad as with the other slot machines.

Just remember: Real men play real Poker. Well, just kidding. Kinda. Real women play real Poker, too.

9

SPORTS BOOK/ SPORTS BETTING

LET ME START THIS topic by indicating something that is already common knowledge for those of you who frequent Atlantic City; legal casino betting on sporting events can only be found in the state of Nevada. (Also, since I don't believe I have mentioned this elsewhere, it is interesting to note that just as Atlantic City does not offer betting on sporting events, it also does not offer either Keno or Poker)

There is no question that betting on sporting events generates more interest and more wagering activity than any other gambling venue. For some reason, a lot of us cannot tolerate watching a sporting event unless we have some "action", a wager to make the contest just a little more interesting. Of course the amount which is illegally wagered in America greatly exceeds the amount which is legally wagered, but should you find yourself in Nevada at a Sports Book, you can make a legal bet.

And not only can you make a legal wager, you can do so in very plush surroundings. Most all of the Sports Books offer large screen televisions, while many of them have numerous large screen televisions, while virtually all of them have numerous small screen televisions. Nearly all Sports Books have comfortable seating, comparable to the best types of theatre or auditorium seating, some with tablet arms for writing and figuring, most with tables, and some of them even have small screen televisions at each seat. The only time you need to move is when you get up to make a wager, but I'm sure this will soon change so that you'll be able to wager from your seat. Should the present trends continue, I wouldn't be surprised to find leather recliners instead of chairs in our future, each connected via computer to the Sports Books' computers, so you need not move at all.

From any seat in the Sports Book, on most any given day, via satellite, you may be able to watch thoroughbred racing from New York, harness racing from Chicago, quarterhorses sprinting in California, and even greyhounds competing in Arizona. If you happen to be there on a Saturday, you may be able to see all of the above, plus a minimum of four or five different college football or basketball games, all at the same time! You'll also see those huge boards, usually white, with the names and associated odds or point spreads for all of the contests for which the Sports Book is accepting wagers. As in the regular casino, there will be attractive waitresses to fetch your drinks, and sometimes food, and at the very least there will usually be a hot dog or deli stand which can serve up your favorite dog or corned beef sandwich without causing you to miss more than a minute from the action. (I must point out here that the very best sandwiches, and especially hot dogs, are usually found in or adjacent to the Sports Book at most casinos. I often find myself lunching in the Sports Book environment, even if I don't have a wager working.)

So let's assume that you want to get away from the Blackjack or Craps tables for a while, or that one of your favorite teams is playing, or that you simply want to experience a Sports Book. Let's further assume that while in the Sports Book, you talk yourself into making a small wager. What are the important things you must know? Actually, very little. You must know how a "Point Spread" works, and you must know how to interpret the "line" or "odds" involved in betting each event. Since the most popular sports, in terms of betting activity, are football and basketball, both college and professional, I'll start with the Point Spread.

Read any major metropolitan newspaper during the football season and you will find, normally at the back of the sports section, a listing of all the major college and professional games which are to be played during that particular week. A typical example might look like this:

Favorite	Points	Underdog
DENVER	7	Chicago
Houston	3	SAN FRANCISCO
NEW ORLEANS	3	Buffalo

This information is interpreted thusly: the Denver Broncos are picked to beat the Chicago Bears by 7 points. The "line" on the game is that Denver is favored by 7 points. Since DENVER is typed in bold caps, this means they are the home team. Houston, playing at San Francisco, is a 3 point favorite, and New Orleans, playing at home, is a 4 point favorite against Buffalo.

In the Sports Book, the large white boards you see behind the wagering counter would reflect the "line", or Point Spreads, by noting the same information like this:

Broncos	-7	Bears	+7
49ers	+3	Oilers	-3
Saints	-4	Bills	+4

Being a fan of the Chicago Bears, I might be interested in wagering, say $50.00 that the Bears will beat the points in this game. Please note that I said I am willing to wager that the Bears will "beat the points in this game". I did not say that the Bears were going to "win" this game. This is because it is not necessary for the Bears to win the game in order for me to win my bet. I am not betting that the Bears will in, I am betting that *either* the Bears will win the game outright, or that should they lose, they will lose by less than 7 points. The +7 behind the Bears name means that when the game is over, for the purposes of my bet, I am going to add 7 points to the final score for the Bears, and that will determine the outcome of my bet. When there is a + "plus" sign behind the team you want to bet, it means that you are "taking" the points. Conversely, a - "minus" sign behind the team you want to bet would mean that you are "giving" the points. To make this wager, I simply walk up to the counter in the Sports Book, give the "teller" my money, and say something like "I'll take the Bears and the seven points." I could also say, "I want the Bears," or any words to that effect.

Using the Broncos and Bears as our example, if the real final score of this game is Broncos 17, Bears 6, the score after adjusting for the points would depend on whether you bet on the broncos or bears. If you took the Broncos, you were "giving" 7 points, which means you must subtract 7 point from their score, making the score for your bet Broncos 10, Bears 6. Obviously, you won. On the other hand, let's say you bet on the Bears, and were therefore "taking" the 7 points, which means you must add 7 points to their score. In this scenario, the final score for purposes of your wager was Broncos 17, Bears 13, and you lost.

Are you with me on this? What if the final real score was, say, Broncos 12, Bears 6, and you bet on the Bears? Did the Bears win? Did you win your bet? Which is more important? The answers: No, Yes, Winning the bet.

Remember that the Point Spread has no effect on the real final score of the game. The Broncos won this game by the score as listed, 12 to 6. Fortunately for us, we were "taking" 7 points with our bet on the Bears, so the final score for our bet was Broncos 12, Bears 13. We win the bet. To address the last question, if you still feel good when the Bears win but you lose money, there is definitely something wrong with you, and you obviously should not be making any wagers, unless someone is willing to bet you utilizing bottle caps or paper clips as tender instead of real money. On the other hand, if you can be happy when you win your bet, even though the Bears lose, you are a normal, well-adjusted American person.

One more example: the real final score is Broncos 13, Bears 6. You took the Broncos, thereby "giving" the 7 points. Who won the game? Who won the bet?

Well, if you were giving 7 points away, the score for your bet is Broncos 6, Bears 6. The Broncos won the game, but nobody won the bet. The bet is a tie or push and nobody wins, nobody loses.

So now we all understand the Point Spread. But you must also know about that $50.00 you were going to wager. Because, you see, the Sports Book is not in business merely to supply all of us with plush surroundings and a good time. It is in business to make money. Can you actually bet $50.00 to win $50.00? No! Think of it this way: In our example, what would happen if exactly 1,000 people bet $50 on the Broncos? The answer is either 1,000 people will be happy, in the case of either team winning with the point spread, or that nobody will be happy, in the case of a tie with the point spread, but for sure the Sports Books was holding $100,000. Regardless of who wins, they must pay out the $100,000, and in the event of a tie, they must return all bets; therefore, they make no money.

How does the Sports Book make their money? All bets are made based on odds of 11 to 10. If you make a bet of $11 and win, you win $10. Your $11 is returned to you, along with the $10 in winnings. We were going to make a bet of $50, remember? Well, we can't do that, because all bets are made in multiples of 11. Consequently, our bet should be $55, which will pay us $50 when we win (actually, we will collect $105, which represents our bet of $55, plus our winnings of $50). A wager of $66 would pay $60, a wager of $22 would pay $20, a wager of $1,100 would pay $1,000, a wager of $770 would pay $700, etc.

Think again about our example where 1,000 people each bet $50 on the Broncos, and another 1,000 bet the Bears for the same amount. Well, we now see that all of those people would really bet $55 each, so now the Sports Book is holding a total of $110,000 ($55,000 +$55,000). The final score of the game is Broncos 10, Bears 7, so all of us Bear supporters won our bet, because the score for our bet is Broncos 10, Bears 14, and all of us who bet $55 are about to have that $55 returned to us, along with another $50 in winnings, so we are going to collect a total of $105. Since there are 1,000 of us who were smart enough to take the points and the Bears, the Sports Book will need to pay out $105 x 1,000 bettors = $105,000. How much were they holding? $110,000. What is their profit? $5,000. And this, folks, is how the Sports Book makes their money. However, you say, what if the game, for purposes if the bets, is a tie? Well, nobody wins, for purposes of the bets is a tie? Well, nobody wins, nobody loses, and the Sports Book makes no money (also known as vigorish). This very seldom happens, and the reason it seldom happens is because every football game ever played will end in a score which involves a whole number. Scores will end in a score which involves a whole number. Scores like 10 to 3, 15 to 6, or 78 to 34. But the Sports Books will seldom post point spreads of whole numbers as I did in our example. The Sports Book will use a point spread which includes one half of a point (1/2). So in our examples of how the point spreads would look on the boards at the Sports Book, they could really look like this:

Broncos	-7 1/2	Bears	+7 1/2
49ers	+3 1/2	Oilers	-3 1/2
Saints	-4 1/2	Bills	+4 1/2

With a point spread that includes a number which is not whole, there can be no ties, insuring that the Sports Book will make the vigorish regardless of the outcome.

This knowledge regarding the Point Spread is all you need to know to make your bet. However, it is interesting to note that the Point Spread is not pulled from some crystal ball, nor based on what any experts feel will really be the final score. Each Sports Book relies on an expert who supplies their answer to this question: At what Point Spread can we ensure that we will receive an equal amount of wagering on both sides of the contest? Stated in other words, the question would read: At what Point Spread can we ensure that $100,000 is wagered on the Broncos, and $100,000 is also wagered on the

Bears? What Point Spread will make all the Bear lovers say to themselves: "I love this spread." while also making all the Bronco lovers say to themselves: "I can't lose with a spread like this."

The expert decides, and these people are unbelievably good at this, that the Broncos should be favored by 8 points. If all the action that the Sports Book gets on the game is being placed on the Bears, the Sports Book must decide if the "line" or Point Spread needs to be changed, or "moved". So they change it to 7 points, and note that more people start taking the Broncos, but they don't want a whole number in the Point Spread, so they make it 7 1/2 and at that point they begin receiving balanced betting on both sides. The line stays at 7 1/2 for the rest of the week. Remember that the expert who came up with this line may really think that the Bears are going to kill the Broncos by at least 37 points, but that is not the issue here. The issue is what Point Spread will bring even wagering on both sides, thereby ensuring that the Sports book protects itself. If the Sports Book received $110,000 from people betting the Bears, and only $11,000 from people betting the Broncos, they would be frantic. They would have collected a total of $121,000, and if the Bears won the bet they would have to pay out a total of $210,000, for a very terrible net loss the the Sports Book of $89,000. Needless to say, the Sports Book would move the line, and keep moving it until the amount of wagers on both sides began to even out. This is why the serious bettor will always shop around for the best Point spreads; they are not always the same at all Sports Books.

Next, we need to understand how to wager on events which are not listed by Point spreads. These other events are ordinarily posted according to Odds.

Have you ever heard anyone say something like "I

wanted the Cubs over the Cardinals, so I had to bet 8 for 5"? What did this mean? Well, it's actually fairly simple, at least at first. What this means is that the odds are 8 to 5, which means that if you bet on the favorite, (in this case the Cubs), you must bet $8.00 to win $5.00. This also means that some expert who is employed by the Sports Book has decided that if the Cubs and Cardinals meet 13 times during the season, the team he has established as the favorite (the Cubs) should win 8 of those contest.

Does this mean that the odds shown on those large white boards will read Cubs 8, Cardinals 5? No. If it reads like that, some people might think they are looking at Point Spreads. Even though you might see number like that in your local paper, you will not see them posted in this manner at the Sports Book. Odds at the Sports Books will be posted based on wagers which will produce a winning amount of $100.00. Our odds on the Cubs and Cardinals of 8 to 5, would have to be changed to an expression of 100, so we must multiply both sides by 20, which means we really have odds of 160 to 100. Yes, this means that a bet of $160 would win $100 if you bet on the Cubs and they win. You heard me right, the Cubs *must* win in order for you to win your bet. When making a bet based on odds, you do not get any help with points. The outcome of your bet is based on the real outcome of the game in question.

Do odds of 160 to 100 mean that you must bet this much? No. I don't mean to confuse you, but odds of 160 to 100 mean that you can bet any amount which is a multiple of the odds stated. So even though I said we had to convert our 8 to 5 odds to an expression of 100, you can actually bet 8 to win 5, or you could bet 16 to win 10, or 40 to win 25, or any other number which is a multiple of the odds. A simple way to figure this out is to add a decimal point to the odds. 160 to 100 then become 1.60 to 1.00, or $1.60 to $1.00. You must bet $1.60 for every $1.00 you want to win. Again, the first number in the odds represents the amount you must wager on the favorite to win a certain amount (160 to 100). In the Sports Book the large whiteboards would show Cubs -160.

Fine, you say. Now I have some idea of what the odds mean if I want to bet on the favorite. But what if I want to bet on the underdog ("dog")? Do odds of 160 to 100 mean that if I want the dog I can bet $100 to win $160? Absolutely not!

Think again in terms of the Sports Book and how they make their money. Using the Cubs and Cardinals at odds of 160 to 100, what if, to keep it very simple, one person bet on the Cubs, and one person on the Cardinals? The Sports Book would then be holding a total of $260. If the Cubs win, they would then need to return that person's $160 wager, plus that person's $100 in winnings, so they would pay back $260, and since they only collected $260, they don't make any money. If the Cardinals win, they still need to return a total of $260, and still don't make any money. Is the Sports Book in business to make money? You bet. So what happens when someone like you wants to bet the dog?

Look again at the odds board. What it will show you is something like this:

Cubs -160 Cardinals +120

What you see is only one number of the odds. The -160 for the Cubs means that they are the favorites and the odds are 160 to 100. The +120 for the Cardinals means that they are the dog and the odds are 100 to 120. That's right, if you want the Cardinals, you will win $120 for every $100 you wager. Sounds better, doesn't it? If you take the Cardinals you win more than you bet.

If you take the Cubs, you win less than you bet. But don't forget that the Cubs should win 8 out of every 13 contests between these two teams. Betting the dog gives you a much better return on your investment, but you may not win a very high percentage of your bets.

Now let's consider the Sports Books' position again. One person bets on the Cubs, one on the Cardinals. The Sports Book is holding $260 (160 +100). The Cubs win. The person who bet the Cubs collects back his bet of $160 plus his winnings of $100 for a total of $260. The Sports Book makes no money.

Change the result. The Cardinals win. The person who bet the Cardinals collects back her bet of $100 plus winnings of $120, for a total of $220. The Sports Book just made a profit of $40.

That's right, when the favorite wins the Sports Book breaks even, when the dog wins the Sports Book makes money. The only thing wrong with my example is that the spread between 160 and 120 is a difference of 40, which you may never see in your life. I used a wide spread to clearly illustrate what we're talking about. In the real world, you will seldom see a difference of more than 15 or 20, and a difference of 10 (also known as a "dime line") is the most prevalent of all.

The house edge on Odds bets starts at about 2% for a dime line, and goes up quickly, so an Odds bet in the Sports Book can be a good one in terms of your disadvantage. Typical odds which you will see posted would look like this:

Cubs	-160	Cardinals	+150
Mets	-130	Padres	+120
Red Sox	-130	Padres	+115

Once you understand Point Spreads and Odds, you can have a try at the Sports Book. You will probably enjoy the surroundings, and for those of you who prefer to watch television this may be the best place in the casino. You can sit there all day, be entertained, and not wager a penny. But why do that? Didn't you come here to gamble in the first place?

Other things to consider at the Sports Book:

1) When you're betting the horses or dogs, your winning wagers are based on the odds which are posted at the track you are betting. If the odds on your horse at Sportsman Park in Chicago are 7 to 1, and the horse wins and pays $16.40 to the bettors in Chicago, you will receive the same $16.40. If the Quiniela pays $56.80 in Chicago, that's what you get.

2) *Don't lose your tickets*! When you make a bet at the Sports Book you will receive a piece of paper called a ticket which will show exactly how you wagered (Win, Place, Show, Chicago, San Francisco, etc.), and the amount of your wager. To collect a winning bet, you must present your ticket. It's no different than at your favorite horse track. Lose, or for that matter destroy your ticket, and you are out of luck. At most Nevada Sports Books your tickets are good for up to a year, and some Sports Books will even cash your ticket by mail. If you misplace a ticket and find it nine months later, there is an excellent chance that it is still collectable.

3) You will find that there are numerous types of wagers which can be made at a Sports Book. I call these wagers "crazy" bets, because, you guessed it, anybody who makes these bets with any frequency is a real looney toon. I am refer-

ring to bets like Parleys, Half Time Bets, Teasers, and Totals. If you want to bet a Parley for $5, it may be worth a try because you could get very lucky. If you want to bet a Parley for $500 you need to talk to a shrink. This is like playing the slot machines. The odds are stacked against you, but it can still be fun to play so long as you are not playing with any of your "serious" gambling money.

10
JUNKETS

WANNA TAKE A TRIP to a casino at nearly no cost to your? Wanna have fun for a day? Has it been a long time since you've visited Nevada, or Atlantic City (or, for that matter, Deadwood, South Dakota, which now has legalized casino gambling)? Do you have gambling fever? Will you soon turn into a raving mad-dog killer, alcoholic misfit, or simply a real severe grouch if you don't get to roll those bones pretty darn soon? Do you dream of getting Blackjacks on every hand, or of beating the dealer with 15s and 16s? Then you need a fix. And since you can't take time off from work right this minute, we're going to give you a shot of a drug called Junket. What is it? What are the side effects? Read on.

A Junket is simply a quick trip to a casino. By "quick", I mean the trip normally consists of one day. You will probably leave your home town by approximately 8:30 in the morning, and return by about 11:00 the same night. Depending upon how far you are from the casino, this will leave you anywhere between nine and thirteen hours of action at the casino. If you need to travel through several time zones to make this trip, you may need to leave earlier in the morning, arrive back later at night, or both. But you will still get in your ten or twelve hours of gambling.

Junkets are sponsored by casinos. The casino will pay some enterprising business person in your area a nominal fee to organize your trip, collect deposits to ensure you make the plane or bus, and keep everybody happy for the full day. Some of these business people are associated with travel agencies, most have diverse occupations. The leader of your group may be your next door neighbor, your mailman, your insurance agent, in short, any person interested in making a little money in their spare time. Or, your junket may be organized by a company which specializes in planning these trips. A company which not only can arrange for you to go to Atlantic City, but can also get you to Elko, Nevada.

The enticing thing about a junket is that it allows you to make this trip at a cost which is much less than what you would ordinarily expect to pay. In exchange for the reduced cost of the trip, you will be expected to gamble at your sponsoring casino for the entire duration of the trip, often at preset minimum wagers. If, for example, the Golden Pearl Casino is sponsoring the trip, they would not want you to get off the plane and head directly for their hated enemy the Black Fate Saloon and Casino. If that's what you want to do, if you want to "cheat" your host casino, probably the worse thing that will happen is that your host will scream at you a little, and stare at you a lot, and you'll never make another trip with this group. But don't be a jerk about this. If the

Golden Pearl is offering a good package, be an honorable person and hold up your end of the bargain. Don't take advantage of a Junket to Carson City, Nevada just because you have an aunt who lives there that you haven't seen in along time.

Here's a few examples of junkets which will easily explain their essence. Since I live near Denver, the examples stem from trips I have made from this area, but these same Junkets are also offered from other cities.

RENO, NEVADA

The cost of this trip (A.K.A. the reservation fee) is currently $35.00. A modern jet is utilized to transport you back and forth. Prior to boarding the plane you must show your host $500 in cash, proof positive that you at least have the money to gamble, whether you in fact gamble or not. You are expected to play all day at this particular casino. You are expected to make minimum wagers of $5 at all table games, and minimum bets of $1 if you are playing slot machines. The group assembles in the reception room of a small, private aviation company. Coffee and donuts await you. An assistant to the host checks to make sure that you are on the list, and that you have already paid your $35. After inquiring as to whether you have a preference for smoking or nonsmoking seating, this person will assign you a specific seat on the plane (don't expect a nonsmoking flight, regardless of the time required for the trip, as this is not considered a commercial flight). You will also receive a badge of some sort which you will be expected to have pinned to a conspicuous place on your clothing for the duration of the Junket. This badge will reflect a number associated with your name. This is how the casino keeps track of who you are and whether you are living up to your end of the deal. Once you have your seat assignment and your badge, you are also given a coupon which is good for either a free buffet lunch, or $5 toward the meal of your choice.

Next, you stand around, or sit, and converse with your fellow passengers. Perhaps, if this is your first trip, you may be a little nervous, so you should ask some of the others if they have made this trip before. Some have, and they put your mind at rest by telling you that this is a small, but first-class, casino which makes every effort to ensure that you will enjoy yourself and come back again.

There is a slight delay in your departure time, because the same jet which is taking you this morning also made a run from Omaha to Reno which left earlier this morning, and it encountered strong head winds crossing Utah. This same jet, by the way, may drop off your group and then make another run to some city further west.

Once you've boarded the aircraft, the host makes a short speech telling you what a good time you're going to have. The plane takes off. There are real stewardesses who come around with drinks and a snack, just like on a real commercial airliner. The host organizes a drawing for cash and other prizes, and you put your $1or $5, or whatever the amount, into the hat in hopes that you'll start the day off lucky. Part of the prizes are distributed on the way to Reno, the rest, including the largest cash prize, are saved for the return trip. The flight takes approximately two hours, but due to the time change we get back one of those hours.

Several buses are waiting for your group at the Reno airport. You file off the plane and immediately onto the buses. The ride to the casino takes only fifteen minutes.

The host, who has now been joined by several casino employees who are goodwill ambassadors, directs you to a room where you can store your coat. The room is locked up, and can you figure out why? Right. If your coat is locked away, it is just a little more difficult for you to leave the casino, particularly if the weather is cold.

You enter the casino, it looks like most nice casinos that you have ever seen before, you play the games of your choice, and before you know it a voice on the public address system is announcing that your bus is now loading and this is the last call. In the meantime, you have met the folks who came in earlier from Omaha, and also those that came in later from Oakland. Whether or not you had a good time may depend upon whether you won or lost money, but you must admit that you were treated fairly by friendly casino employees.

This, folks, is a very typical trip. Here are some other options available from Denver.

LAUGHLIN, NEVADA

Basically the same package as the one to Reno. $35.00 reservation fee, meal ticket to the buffet, show $350 cash, $5 minimum table games, $1 minimum slot play. Leave at about 9:00 AM, back home about midnight. I should also point out, by the way, that just because the casino wants you to make $5 minimum wagers does not mean that someone will break your arm if your don't. If you want to make $2 wagers, go ahead. Only, don't expect to be allowed to make the next trip. However, it is possible that you will be allowed back. Remember, you have that badge on your shirt or blouse. If you make $2 wagers all day, but play hard and steady for nine or ten hours and drop three of four hundred, the casino will probably know it, and you can come right on back the next time.

CARSON CITY, NEVADA

Same program as the two listed above.

ELKO, NEVADA

Same kind of deal as the three listed above.

Incidentally, some of you may be thinking: "Who in their right mind would ever consider making a trip to some place like Elko, Nevada, which can't possibly be more than a tiny pitstop on some two-lane highway out in the middle of the desert?" Some of you may not want to go anywhere except Atlantic City, Las Vegas, or Reno. To those of you who think like that, I say: "Is Florida the only place in the world where you can get sunshine in December?" Of course not! Even though Elko is a small town, the highway is four-lane and major, the casinos have all the class of a Las Vegas strip casino, they are just a tad smaller. So don't turn your nose up at the idea of a Junket just because it's not going to a "major" or "name" destination. Don't ignore blonds just because you know you like redheads.

How did I discover these junkets? I found most of them advertised in either the travel section of the Sunday newspaper, or in the sports section on most any day. Once you take a trip with a junket operator, you will automatically be on their mailing list every time they design a new junket.

What about a trip from Chicago to Atlantic City? Here is how one such trip operates: Your reservation fee starts at about $120, and could go up to about $160 depending on whether you travel during the week or on a weekend (obviously, the amount of the reservation fee would be subject to change if this Junket company is using regular commercial flights). Like all the others, you depart early AM, return late PM. The rest is slightly different from the trips I described earlier. Instead of charging only a nominal reservation fee, as noted above, you pay out between $120 and $160. But does the trip really cost you this much? No. Here's why. This Junket returns to you all of the following: Your round trip airfare, $20 in cash, $20 worth of food vouchers a $20 voucher which can be applied to a future trip, a $15 show and free cocktail, a $10 voucher for the bus trip from and to the airport, and a free gift of unknown value from the casino. If your reservation fee was $120, and you subtract the value of all these bonuses, the actual cost of this trip is only about $35.

BUS FROM YOUR EAST COAST TOWN TO ATLANTIC CITY

There are numerous East Coast towns which offer a bus to Atlantic City for a nominal reservation fee. Most of these operate like the trip I described to Reno, except that you are traveling by bus instead of by airplane.

Does a Junket always last for one day? No. Though I tend to think of junkets as group plans, you can also arrange to stay for several days under some plans and basically travel on your own instead of with a group. For example, several casinos are currently offering a Junket whereby you pay for your own airfare, and arrive and depart by your own schedule. You must gamble for a certain time period at a certain minimum bet, which qualifies you for some goodies. Naturally, the goodies vary depending on the nature of your wagers. The $5 bettor can qualify for free drinks anywhere in the casino, free shows, free buffet meals, and a cash allowance which will cover the cost of the room. Added together, these perks make the actual cost of the trip the equivalent of the cost of the airfare only. All this $5 bettor has to do is play for a minimum of 8 hours during his stay of two or three nights. These perks used to be offered only to high rollers, those being "comped" by the casino. Due to the changing nature of the gambling business, the picture is beginning to look brighter for a lot of us. The casinos are getting a little tired of fighting each other for the true high rollers, and have discovered that their meat and potatoes are provided by gamblers like you and me who arrive with a stake of $1,000 and play hard for a couple of days. They still want the high rollers, but they need you and me to be successful and they are finally giving us access to the type of programs previously reserved only for the person willing to wager $50 and up per hand. Of course us little guys aren't going to get the best of the suites, or the gourmet meals, or preferred seating at the shows, but we can still have a good time.

As you can see by these examples, there are several options available to us that more or less fall into the Junket category. We can make a short trip at very little cost and satisfy out urges to gamble. Are there pitfalls to beware? Just a couple.

The single thing I like the least about a Junket is that I am forced to stay at that one casino regardless of how I am doing. As I have stated earlier in this book if you are not doing well at one table, move to another. If you are not doing well at one casino, move to another. Well, when on a Junket that may not be easy to do. You can stop gambling, but then it's kind of boring to just sit in a casino all day with no action.

The second thing I don't like about a Junket is that I have nowhere to go should I want to take a nap, a swim, or a break of some kind. Yes, I can go to the coffee shop, or in some cases I can go to the Sports Book, but when I am gambling hard I sometimes need a nap, and I don't have anywhere to take one when I am on a Junket of the one day variety.

Other than the two limitations just mentioned, I hardily recommend that you try a Junket. Perhaps I have been fortunate, but all of the Junkets I've tried have been well organized and honest.

The one thing, however, that you should do is ask a few questions before sending in your reservation fee. What kind of plane is being used? Is the plane supplied by a company licensed to provide these types of flights? What minimum bets are required? What are the Blackjack rules? Single deck, double deck, or shoe? Is there a Poker Room, and does Poker qualify on this trip? Can you be provided with a list of happy prior customers? If not, can the Junket operator have a satisfied customer call you? What provision has been made in case you need to stay overnight due to weather or airplane malfunction? How long has the junket operator been scheduling trips to any casinos?

I'm sure you get my drift. So, if you need that quick fix, try out a one day junket. It could be just the remedy you need.

11

RED DOG

ALTHOUGH THE CASINOS call this game Red Dog, most of you have probably already heard of it under names such as Acey-Duecey, In-Between, Between the Sheets, or Split the Sheets. This is a game which may have been played by your great grandfather if he was a cowboy or miner, or a man who frequented the bars of the wild west back in the 1800's. The rules are extremely simple and the game can be fun to play, even though this is another game where the odds are stacked heavily against you.

Red Dog tables are generally found adjacent to, in the middle of, or somewhere close to the Blackjack tables. It is played on a Blackjack table, but the felt reflects a different layout. There is a dealer. There is a shoe containing at least six decks. You begin by placing a wager. The dealer exposes two cards by placing them face up in front of his position. The question is: Will the value of the next card off the deck fall between the value of the two exposed cards? Aces are always high, Deuces are always low. If there is no spread between the first two cards, like a Nine and a Ten, there is an automatic tie, you neither win nor lose, and a new round begins. Before the dealer exposes the third card, you have a decision to make: You can leave your wager as it is, or you can double it. That's right, you really only have two decisions in this game. First, you must decide on the size of your initial wager. Second, you must decide whether to double your wager.

On those occasions when the first two cards exposed by the dealer are the same (a pair), you cannot double your bet. (Don't worry, you can't lose if this happens.) The dealer draws a third card to see if three of a kind can be made. If three of a kind is not made, you have a tie, or push, and a new round begins. Should the third card make three of a kind, the players are all paid off at the rate of 11 to 1. This sounds very nice, except that the true payoff for this wager should be 24 to 1.

The payoffs for all other bets are dependent upon the spread between the first two cards. A one-card spread (Jack-King) pays off at 5 to 1. A two-card spread (Jack-Ace) pays off at 4 to 1. A three-card spread (Ten-Ace) pays off at the rate of 2 to 1, and any spread higher than three pays off at even money. If you need clarification on this, the Jack-Ace create a 2-card spread, because there are only two cards which fall between a Jack and an Ace, namely the King and the Queen. The dealer always announces the size of the spread, gives you a moment to decide whether to double your wager, and then deals the third card.

To keep yourself out of trouble in this game, study the chart, below, while keeping in mind the payoffs listed above. Those of you who are interested can determine the house edge on your own. I'll merely state that it is very high. Yes, you do benefit by being able to double your wager in favorable situations, but even if you cut the house edge in half, you're still better off playing Roulette. However, this is another one of those games which can be fun to play, so at least give yourself a chance by studying this chart.

Spread	Win %	Lose %	True Odds
0	4%	96%	24-1
1	8%	92%	11 1/2-1
2	16%	84%	5 1/4-1
3	24%	76%	3-1
4	32%	68%	2-1
5	40%	60%	1 1/2-1
6	48%	52%	1-1
7	52%	48%	1-1
8	60%	40%	1-1 1/2

Here is how I came up with these figures. Consider a spread of 4. The first two cards are a Seven and a Queen. We determine the odds by thinking of this as a one-deck game in which only two cards have been dealt. Starting with 52 cards in the deck, we now have only 50 left because one of the Seven and one of the Queens have already been played. We must draw either an Eight, a Nine, A ten or a Jack to be a winner. There are four of each of these cards in the deck, so there are 16 total chances of us winning. All of the rest of the cards in the deck will cause us to lose, so we have 34 chances of losing. The number of winning chances divided by the total number of chances (16 divided by 50), gives us our percentage of winning. The ratio of winning chances (16) to losing chances (34) can be determined by dividing 16 into 34, for a result of 2.13, which I listed as 2 in the chart, or odds of 2-1.

It does not take superior intellect to figure out that your best chances of winning and collecting on proper odds is when the spread is at least 6. Whenever you have a spread of 6 or more, you should definitely double your bet.

I am sure that some of you are thinking that those of us who can count cards should have an easy time of it in this game. After, all, if we know that a high number of ten-value cards have been played, and we have a spread that needs a ten-value card, we should not double our wager. Conversely, when we have a spread of only 3 or 4 which requires a ten-value, we may want to double if the shoe is abundant with ten-values, even though the chart indicates that the odds are against us. So, yes, counting can definitely help.

Unfortunately, since the spread changes on every hand, and since the exact cards required also changes, counting cards does not help as much as you would hope. For example, a spread of 4 on this hand could be Six-Jack, then on the next hand it might be Two-Seven, and then again it might be Nine-Ace. Counting cards might aid us in the case of the Two-Seven hand or the Nine-Ace hand, but the Six-Jack hand is still up for grabs.

The real key to this game is to know what the spread will be before you make your initial bet. I suppose a really good counting system would help solve this problem, but I have yet to discover it. I hope you do. Until then, keep your wagers at the minimum and double only when the odds are on your side. Losing $$ is one thing, donating it is another.

12

WHEEL OF FORTUNE/ BIG WHEEL

TRUST ME on this one, okay? Don't play this game.

13

FATE, LUCK, AND INTUITION

LET ME TELL YOU A STORY. One day a few years ago I decided to visit a local greyhound track for one of my frequent attempts at parimutual wagering. While driving on my way to the track I turned on the radio. The station was conducting a live interview with a well known athlete who is known locally as T.J. I listened for approximately seven minutes, then hit my station selector. What did I hear next? A newsman reading a story that involved this same athlete with the initials T.J., followed by an advertisement for a company whose name starts with the letters T.J. What was the very next billboard I saw adjacent to the highway? An advertisement for the same company whose advertisement is still running on the radio.

Six or seven minute later I reach the track. I'm arriving late, so it's almost time for the tenth race. I buy a program. What name do I see, a name which because of what I've seen and heard jumps out at me like a jack-in-the-box? Right! A greyhound whose name starts with the initials T.J. Do I have enough time to study the program before placing a bet? No. Do I decide that all the T.J.s from the last twenty-five minutes are more than coincidence? Of course. So I bet this T.J. dog on top in the trifecta, he wins and keys a payoff of about $900.

Was this just luck on my part? Was it fate? Was it intuition? Probably a little of each.

Obviously this story has nothing to do with casino gambling, but I relate it because it emphasizes the point that I want to make in this chapter, which is this: In addition to having knowledge of basic systems and odds, you must be aware of what is happening to you and around you. What is happening to and around you will provide you with strong clues as to whether luck or fate are on your side, and whether your intuition has taken a winter vacation in Iceland.

You are playing Blackjack. The twenty you receive on your first hand looks great since the dealer is showing a Six. The dealer's down card is a Seven, she hits and gets a Three, she hits again and catches a Five. Twenty-one beats twenty. You lose. The dealer had two chances to bust. First when she hit a hard thirteen, again when she hit a hard sixteen.

You play another hand, the twenty you receive on this hand looks every bit as good as the twenty on the hand before, but now the dealer is showing a Ten so you don't have quite the confidence you did on the first hand. Your hopes increase when the dealer reveals a Four for a down card, your eyes widen with delight when the dealer draws an Ace, and then you collapse back onto your chair when she hits again and catches a Six. Again, twenty-one beats twenty. Again, you lose. Again, the dealer had to take two hits, either of which could have busted her hand but didn't.

You play again. Being the impatient type, you pick up your first card almost before it hits the felt, and it's an Ace. Even better, the second card is a ten-value and you now have Blackjack. So does the dealer. Blackjack ties a Blackjack, so you didn't lose. Maybe you should stick around for another hand.

Are you crazy? What is happening to you? Think about it. You're losing, yes, but how are you losing? You are getting great hands, but not winning with them. Does someone need to smack you over the head? STOP PLAYING! Change tables or change casinos. At times, how you lose is just as, if not more, important than the fact that you lose.

The casino next door smells good when you walk in. You can't identify the odor, but it suits your senses. Maybe things will improve, you think. Well, tough luck. Your first hand of Blackjack is a wonderful combination of a Seven and a Nine. You now have one foot in the grave. The dealer is showing a Nine. You're probably dead meat on this one. What is the dealer's down card? Take that one foot of yours back out of the grave. The dealer exposes a Six, then draws a beautiful, oh so beautiful Seven. Your sixteen beats her twenty-two.

That scent you keep sniffing is smelling better all the time. Betting two units becomes a thought that you act on almost before you realize you're doing it. An Eight and a Three show up on your first two cards. The dealer is showing a Four. You begin to lick your lips. Instead of two units, you wish you had bet two hundred units. You double down. The dealer slips you a card face down. An excited, trembling left hand which is connected to your body reaches out and turns it over. It's the Two of Clubs, and you feel a sharp pain in your stomach. Now you wish you had stayed with a one unit wager. The dealer exposes a Seven, for a total of eleven, and you are thinking "here we go again, right down the drain", but the dealer's net card is an Ace, then a Three, and whammo, a Ten. Thirteen beats twenty-five. You win. The dealer had three chances to make a hand, but didn't.

What is happening to you? Of course you are winning, but how are you winning? You are winning hands that you should be losing, hands that you will lose the overwhelming majority of the time. Does someone need to smack you over the head and tell you to recognize that this may be the start of something wonderful? That you had better start thinking in terms of jacking up those bets?

Being slightly timid, you stay with only a two unit bet. You are dealt a marvelous thirteen. The dealer is showing a King. The basic system says to hit. You haven't been counting, so you should play the basic system. But, yet, somehow your gut feeling, your intuition tells you to stand. You know it's not a smart play. In fact it's downright ignorant. Except that it works. The dealer has a five for a down card and draws an Eight. Thirteen beats twenty-three. You win again.

You are convinced that fate or luck is smiling upon you, so you wisely institute a progressive betting system and you do very well. Congratulations! You weren't simply playing, you were also being aware of what was taking place. The winning of hands that you should be losing is one of the strongest indicators of the birth of a winning streak.

On another occasion you are playing Pai Gow Poker. You win the first hand. You lose the second hand. You win the third hand. You lose the fourth hand. You win the fifth hand. You lose the sixth hand. Does anyone see a pattern here? If you experienced a pattern like this, would you be aware enough to recognize it? Would you do anything about it? Could you maybe bet one unit on the even hands and then boost your bet up to fifteen or twenty units on the odd hands? If a floorman came over to the table and stared at you, would you shrug and tell him that you've been winning every other hand? Why not? It's the truth. The dealer will confirm what you tell the floorman, and you will not have a problem.

Back to Blackjack. You're at third base. With the dealer showing a Six, the woman sitting adjacent to you splits a pair of Tens and receives two more. You stand pat on your thirteen. The dealer's down card is an Eight. Either one of the last two cards off the deck would have busted the dealer had this trash bag next to you stayed with her original twenty like she should have. The dealer catches a Seven and everybody at the table loses.

On the next hand the dealer shows a Six. Your total is eleven. The mess next to you has fifteen. Before you can tell her you'll bread her fingers if she tries to hit, she busts her hand with a Queen. You still double down and receive the Eight that would have gone to the dealer had El Bimbo played her hand correctly. The dealer exposes a Jack as his down card, draws a Three, and you're down the tubes again. If this woman doesn't draw, you end up with twenty-one and the dealers busts. Are you aware of what is happening? This is bad luck and perhaps bad fate as well. Move on.

Conversely, what if the woman next to you made all these ignorant moves, and you won because of it? Would that be good? Absolutely. Would this be a good sign? Guess for yourself.

Give Craps a try. Bet the Pass Line. The shooter is hot. She tosses a seven on the comeout, then makes her point of four. However, there is a man at the table who has been tossing, scattering, and just plain dropping chips all over the table. He claims to have a winner on every throw, whether he actually has one or not. He is quite obnoxious. In fact he is skunk-odorous. Before you know it, one of the dealers, the stickman and the boxman are all being called various nasty names by this guy. They are not enchanted by this man's demeanor. You can see their lips tightening, their faces begin to flush. The shooter's next roll is a pair of sixes. The dice move to the next roller, but so long as Mr. Personality continues to give the pit crew a rough time, nobody can make a pass.

Keep this in mind. For some reason, whenever one of the players at your table is upsetting the dealer, stickman, or whomever is controlling that particular game, you may as well move along. Be aware of what is happening to and around you.

Given the situation I just described at the Crap table, would you be sharp enough to either 1) leave the table, or 2) start betting the Don't Pass?

Remember that these examples have nothing whatsoever to do with the science of gambling. They have to do with luck, fate and intuition.

Here is something which I do out of habit, because I discovered a long time ago that this action helps me. Whenever I change tables, I always take my chips to the cashier's cage, cash them, and buy new chips when I play again. I do this because I observed during one three-night stay that virtually every time I switched tables and played with existing chips, I lost. Every time I switched tables and did not play until after seeing the cashier, I improved. Note that I did not say I won. I improved my play. I may still have lost, but at a slower rate. Some people might think this is just pure luck. Others may analyze this and say that the time it takes me to walk to the cashier's cage and then back to the tables give me time to collect myself before continuing play. Whatever the case, it works for me.

All of us, I am sure, have at least some regard for fate, luck, and intuition. But even if you don't believe in any of the three, doesn't it make sense to be aware of what is happening to and around you? And doesn't it make very good sense to make modifications in your gambling when you notice that certain incidents tend to help or hinder you? Of course it does. Combine awareness with a sound system of play, and you're sure to find that a pleasant fate visits you frequently, that lady luck smiles a little, and that your intuition is more keen.

14 PRACTICAL ADVICE

THIS CHAPTER is a collection of tips which can mean the difference between success and failure in Atlantic City, Las Vegas, or other gambling meccas. You cannot enter a casino and rely on blind luck to protect your money or make you a winner. Though blind luck has probably won more money than all the gambling systems combined, blind luck is not consistent. If lady luck is on you side during your next gambling session, you can do everything wrong and still win. But if lady luck deserts you, you must take steps to protect yourself against disastrous losses. You don't want to lose your entire gambling stake in the first few hours of the trip and then spend the rest of your time swearing at yourself. If you follow all of the advice contained in this chapter, one of two things will happen:

1) You will substantially reduce your losses.

2) You might even win.

Some of my suggestions have already been covered in earlier chapters, but all warrant repeating.

MONEY MANAGEMENT

1) Divide your gambling fund into two groups. Eighty percent or more should be serious money, twenty percent or less should be fun money.

2) Start with at least fifty units of serious money. One hundred units is ideal.

3) Do not lose more than five units at any table: Blackjack, Craps, Roulette or Baccarat. Change tables before you lose more. If there aren't any more tables, change casinos. Often, being at a new table or casino will brighten your outlook and sharpen your judgment.

4) If you win as many as ten units, do not lose it back.

5) If you win as many as twenty-five units, increase your unit. Then if you win another fifteen units, increase your unit again.

6) Do not forget that you're playing for real money, not chips. Each time the dealer collects one of your green chips, you've lost $25. Chips are money!

7) Above all else, do not gamble with money you can't afford to lose.

BETTING STRATEGY

Stay at a minimum wager until you start winning. Do not chase good money with bad money. Increasing your bets will not change the cards or dice.

Once you find yourself in a position where your winnings total 40 or 50 units, you may want to try a progressive betting system to help maximize your profits. Here's one I happen to like: Start with a minimum wager. If you win, bet the minimum again. If you win again, double your bet. If you win again, collect your winnings but leave out the same bet (double the minimum). If you then win again, double your bet again. After that the process is drag (collect your winnings but not the bet), *then* press (double your bet), then drag, press, drag, press, until your luck changes. If you lose, go back to your minimum wager and start again.

If you start with a one-unit bet, your wagers would look like this: 1, 1, 2, 2, 4, 4, 8, 8, 16, 16, and so on. Using this betting system, you're trying for three consecutive wins. If you lose the second bet you break even. If you win the second bet, every succeeding bet adds to your profits without jeopardizing any of your gambling stake. The system is designed to take advantage of any hot streaks you encounter, maximizing your winnings.

Of course, if you start with a high unit, say $50, and you win several consecutive hands, you quickly exceed the maximum bet allowed at most tables. If this happens, do not remain at the maximum bet. Instead, start all over again with a minimum wager.

Example: Your betting unit is $50. You win the first hand, so you collect your winnings of $50 and leave your original bet of $50 out for the next round. You win again, but this time you press (add your $50 in winnings to your original bet of $50) for a total bet of $100. You win again, so you drag (remove your winnings, but remain with your last bet). You win again, so you press again (add your winnings to your bet), making your new bet $200. If you win again, you drag $200 and leave the bet at $200. Another win would press your bet to $400, where it would stay for two hands. Then you would bet $800 for the following two hands. But if the table limit is $1,000, you would then drop back down to your original wager of $50. Here's what your bets look like:

Place table here

Seldom, if ever, will you win so many consecutive hands, but if it happens, you should be prepared to take advantage and maximize your profits. In addition, even if you were only to win five or six hands in a row, you've still maximized your winnings and profits.

But, you ask, what happens if I'm playing Blackjack and my sixth hand is a total of 11 and the dealer is showing a Six? Should I double down? My answer is no. Again, you shouldn't get overly greedy. Doubling your bet at that point would cause a loss of the majority of your winnings. Why win five or six hands in a row and not have any profits to show for your streak? The idea of this system is to keep playing with the casino's money — this is, money which does not come from our gambling stake. Also, remember that I indicated that you would not use this system until *after* you had already won 40 or 50 units. So, in general, when you're using this type of progressive betting system in Blackjack, forget about doubling down and splitting.

I once observed my wife winning fifteen consecutive hands of Blackjack. Unfortunately, she refused to increase her bets. Had she used this betting system she would have won 127 units instead of 15.

When you're losing, you don't want to lose more than one unit at a time. When you're winning, you want to win *multiple* units each time.

CARD COUNTING

If you're counting cards while playing Blackjack, do not increase your bets too much when the deck is rich. Staying within a range of one to three units will keep you out of trouble; betting one unit when the deck is poor, three units when it is rich.

Six years ago, I was asked to leave a Blackjack table. I was varying my bets from $5 to $100 depending on the count. In essence, I was saying to the casino, "Look at me! I'm counting and winning your money!" Yes, I was stupid. I was winning so much that I became overconfident, cocky. Had I controlled my bets properly, I would've won more money and the casino would've thought I was just lucky.

RULE VARIATIONS

Do not play at casios where the rules are unfavorable to the player. From reading the rule variations in the earlier chapters, you know that some casinos have more liberal rules than others. Why gamble at a casino which insists on stacking the odds against you? Take a few hours to seek out the casinos which offer the best rules for the players; your time will be well spent.

ALCOHOL

If you're going to let the casino feed you free drinks, exercise restraint. How can you remember proper gambling methods and protect your money if you can't even remember what day it is? Do your drinking while toying with your fun money. Better yet, do your drinking a any time *except* when you're gambling.

COMFORT

In some casinos the Blackjack tables are so close together that it is impossible to find a comfortable chair. How can you concentrate on gambling when the adjacent player's elbow is banging into your ribs? How can you concentrate when the man behind you keeps pushing his chair into yours? Better yet, how can you concentrate when the lovely lady (or handsome man, if you're a lady) next to you has her leg firmly planted against yours? Find a chair with some room around it.

TIME

There aren't any clocks in the casinos, so wear a watch. If your game plan calls for one-hour gambling sessions, you need a way to tell when the hour has passed.

INTIMIDATION

Some casino employees (dealers, pit bosses, floorpersons, and others) tend to intimidate some gamblers. Do not allow yourself to be intimidated. Don't worry if a pit boss looks at you as though you're doing something wrong — that's the way they always look. To some casino employees, every gambler is a cheater out to rip off the casino. Do not feel uncomfortable just because you're winning and the floorman is staring at you, peeking over your shoulder, or trying to distract you. He is really just trying to do his job. If you talk to the employees you'll find that most of them are very nice, very polite, and very helpful.

TIPPING

There is only one time when you should tip a dealer: if the dealer has worked to make your gambling enjoyable. He or she then deserves a tip. I realize that dealing is a difficult job, but some dealers are so obnoxious that they deserve to be locked in a cage full of gorillas. Some dealers are so discourteous that they belong on an island of lepers. However, there are more good dealers than bad. Tip the good ones and ask the bad ones why they didn't have human parents.

Note: If you find a particularly enjoyable dealer, and if that same dealer is winning every four out of five hands, change tables. Don't stay at a losing table simply because you like the dealer.

REST

Most of us can only stay mentally alert when we are well rested. I know that it's difficult to nap or sleep while you're in such an exciting environment, but try to get as much rest as you can. In addition, try to refresh your body and mind with physical exercise: a game of tennis or a few laps in the beautiful swimming pools. Take frequent breaks to remove your mind from gambling.

Try to do your gambling an hour or two at a time. However, there is an exception to this rule. If you find yourself in a situation where the composition of the deck or the "run" of the dice, combined with your playing ability, is proving very lucrative, then give yourself a little more time. Why walk away from a table when you're winning? No, I'm not saying that if you're winning one unit, you should stay at that table. I'm saying that if you're winning, say, thirty to fifty units, you should stay right where you are *as long as you continue to win.* If you start to lose back a portion of your winnings, say as much as five to seven units, or if you're winning, but starting to feel exhausted, move on to the hotel's steam room.

PRACTICE

Before starting your holiday, practice your specialty. One reading of this book or any other book is not enough. You *must* practice the game or games you plan to play. You must have *in-depth* knowledge of your specialty. You don't become a winning tennis professional by reading a book on tennis. Likewise, you can't become a winning gambler by reading a book on gambling. You must practice, practice, practice. Start refreshing your memory a few weeks before you depart for Las Vegas, Reno, or Atlantic City. An hour or two of practice each day should suffice.

SELF-CONTROL

None of my suggestions mean anything unless you have the discipline required to use them. You must not let emotions dictate your play. You must be able to control yourself. You can do anything you want — with your fun money. But when gambling with your serious money, you must control yourself.

Note: I do not mean to imply that you should not have any fun. If you only gamble with your serious money six hours each day, you only need to control yourself for six hours each day. For the other eighteen hours of each day you can get drunk, be a clown, be a fool, be a lover, or be a blithesome idiot if you want. Have fun with your fun money and exercise control with your serious money. You'll have an enjoyable *and* profitable time.

CASINO ADVANTAGE

Throughout this book I've listed the various casino advantages on the different wagers available to you. Now, to give added meaning to those cold figures, I'll talk real dollars and cents.

Example 1: You are a $5 bettor, playing roulette. On every spin of the wheel you bet on either red or black. The casino advantage is 5.26%. You play for three days, averaging twelve hours of playing time each day. The Roulette wheel spins approximately forty times each hour. How much money can you expect to lose?

Here is how to figure it out: Forty bets per hour time twelve hours times three days, equals 1,440 total bets. At $5 per bet, you would then wager a total of $7,200! In gambling parlance, this would be termed $7,200 worth of "action." And if we multiply $7,200 by the casino advantage of 5.26%, we find that you could expect to lose $378.72.

Since you expect to lose only $378, does this mean that you could start play with a bankroll (gambling stake) of only, say, $500? Absolutely not! You might very well lose $900 the first day, win back $300 the second day, and then win another $222 the third day.

Example 2: You are still a $5 bettor, but now you are playing craps, betting on the field. The casino advantage is 11.2% Field bets are one-roll wagers, so you win or lose on every roll of the dice. You play for three days, you stay at the tables for twelve hours each day, making approximately sixty bets per hour.

Sixty bets per hour times twelve hours times three days equals 2,160 total bets. At $5 per bet, you would wager a total of $10,800. And $10,800 multiplied by the casino advantage of 11.2% would mean losses of $1,209.60.

Example 3: You are playing craps again, still a $5 bettor, but this time you are a little smarter. Since you know the casino advantage on the Pass Line is only 1.4%, that is your bet. Also, you are now making fewer bets per hour, because it often takes numerous rolls of the dice to determine whether you win or lose. So, we'll say you only make thirty bets per hour.

Thirty bets per hour times twelve hours times three days equals 1,080 total bets. At $5 per bet, your total action would be $5,400. $5,400 multiplied by the casino advantage of 1.4% would equal losses of $75.60

Of course you could have gotten lucky and actually won money in one of these examples, but the odds are against you. Plus, the worse the odds are, the less chance you have of experiencing consistent wins.

A hard question: In the future, now that you know the odds and the casino's advantages, which of the games will you play with your serious money, and what bets will you make? If your answer is that you want to be like the person in Examples 1 and 2 above, buying this book was a waste of your money. But if your answer is that you want to be like the person in Example 3, there is definite hope for you.

In Example 3 you have plenty of action, gamble for a long time, have plenty of fun, and lose a minimal share of your gambling stake. Also, since the casino advantage in Example 3 is so narrow, you have a good chance of experiencing winning sessions.

Be smart! Protect your money.

Good luck!

RECOMMENDED READING

How to Win at Blackjack, Charles Einstein. Gambler's Book Club, Las Vegas, 1979.

Scarne on Cards: How to Win at Poker, Gin, Pinochle, Black Jack, Hearts, Cribbage, & Other Games, rev. ed., John Scarne. Crown Publishers, New York, 1974.

Playboy's Guide to Casino Gambling: Craps, Blackjack, Roulette, & Baccarat, Edwin Silberstang. Playboy Press, Chicago, 1980.

Beat the Dealer: A Winning Strategy for the Game of Twenty-One, rev. ed., Edward O. Thorp. Random House, New York, 1966.